THE CHRISTIAN HERITAGE OF OUR NATION

HISTORY CURRICULUM - Ten National Landmarks

Catherine Millard, D. Min.

Illustrator: Maxwell Edgar

Illustrator: Maxwell Edgar

Grateful acknowledgments:
To Mrs. Florian Thayn, Head of Art and Reference, Office of the Architect of the Capitol, for her invaluable assistance and encouragement during the many years of study and research in formulating this book from original sources.

Published by **Christian Heritage Ministries**
Distributed by **Christian Heritage Tours, Inc.**
6597 Forest Dew Court
Springfield, Virginia 22152
Telephone: 703-455-0333

Printed in the United States of America

Definitions of terms used frequently in the text:

Symbol—Something that stands for, or represents another thing; especially an object used to represent something abstract; an emblem; as, the dove is a symbol of peace, the cross is the symbol of Christianity.

Landmark—An event considered a high point or turning point of a period.

Monument—Something set up to keep alive the memory of a person or event, as a tablet, statue, pillar, building, etc.; a writing or the like serving as a memorial; a work, production, etc., of enduring value or significance; as, monuments of learning; vb. . .to erect a monument to the memory of; as to monument a noble deed.

Memorial—Anything meant to help people remember some person or event, as a statue, holiday, etc. (e.g. Exodus 3:15; 17:14; Joshua 4:7; Acts of the Apostles 10:4)

Aesthetics—The theory of the fine arts and of peoples' responses to them; the science or that branch of philosophy which deals with the beautiful; the doctrines of taste.

(Webster's New 20th Century Dictionary— Unabridged—Second Edition)
Scripture parallels for the term "Memorial" added.

Cover Photograph: *Embarkation of the Pilgrims at Delft Haven, Holland, July 22, 1620,* by Robert W. Weir. Photo by John W. Wrigley.

DEDICATION

To the United States of America, a country which opened its arms wide to me in my hour of need, and where I found the Pearl of Great Price -- the Lord Jesus Christ.

THE CHRISTIAN HERITAGE OF OUR NATION

HISTORY CURRICULUM - Ten National Landmarks

TABLE OF CONTENTS

INTRODUCTION

While studying the inception and historical development of this great nation from original sources, it has been an amazing discovery to find that all current literature, including textbooks, history books, guidebooks and brochures pertaining to our blessed country have been robbed of their accuracy. Let me explain. In the earliest documentation we have on record at the Library of Congress of the United States, up through approximately 60 to 70 years ago, Christianity is woven into the warp and woof of this nation's history. The framers of the Constitution turned to Scripture and prayer for guidance in formulating a new system of government, while most of America's greatest leaders, statesmen and inventors gave all glory to Almighty God, as the source and strength of their power and ability.

The need for this curriculum is urgent, as we are now evidencing the removal of tangible items of our precious American Christian heritage from national landmarks, monuments, memorials and shrines where the hand of God in the affairs of this nation is so boldly proclaimed.

Hence, the removal of America's true history from the hearts and minds of today's youth – the leaders of tomorrow. More importantly, God's glory, and that of His Son Jesus Christ in the foundations of America, is being removed. As founding father Thomas Jefferson wrote more than 200 years ago: "Can the liberties of a nation be secure when we have removed the conviction that these liberties are the gift of God? I tremble for my country when I reflect that God is just and that His justice cannot sleep forever."

The Purpose for this curriculum is to inculcate and perpetuate these great landmarks of America's Christian heritage and history in the hearts and lives of present-day youth, in order that they, in turn, may emulate the lives and deeds of great American statesmen and heroes in adulthood.

The Inception and Development of our Capital City

Let us begin at the beginning:

In 1608 the area which now boasts the nation's capital, and one of the world's greatest power centers, was discovered by Captain John Smith. George Washington chose this site himself in 1790 for the new federal city. At that time it lay mid-way between the northernmost and southernmost states. A year later, Washington appointed a French engineer by the name of Pierre Charles l'Enfant, who had served under him in the Revolutionary War, to draw up a plan for the new city. This imaginative, avant garde designer mapped out the streets in a simple but practical manner. From the Capitol, he numbered the streets running north to south, lettering those which ran from east to west. Broad avenues, bearing the names of the states, run crosswise in a diagonal pattern. The original lands were a gift from the states of

Virginia and Maryland. In 1846, however, Virginia took back her portion of land, making the present-day total area of the District of Columbia 69 square miles.

Letters and notes accompanying l'Enfant's plans show a definite purpose in every aspect of his design. He wrote:

> a street laid out on a dimension proportioned to the greatness which the capital of a powerful Empire ought to manifest . . .[1]

The magnificence of Versailles prompted Enfant's grandiose ideas for the young nation's capital.[2] His broadest avenue of 400 feet has now become the grassy expanse separating the northern and southern rows of buildings which comprise the Smithsonian Institution.[3] A unique privilege of excelling the height of the Capitol's dome was granted the Washington Monument. At 555 feet, 5 and one eighth inches, the obelisk serves to salute the father and founder of this nation. An aluminum cap atop the national monument shouts out its own song of praise and worship to our God and Father. An inscription upon it bears the Latin words *Laus Deo*, that is to say, "Praise be to God."

In 1800, the government moved from Philadelphia to Washington with its 126 workers, 32 Senators and 106 Representatives. Before the move, eight other capitals had been evidenced as follows: Albany, New York, Philadelphia, Baltimore, York, Princeton, Annapolis and Trenton.

Since *God's Signature over the Nation's Capital* was published ten years ago, we have evidenced, at a cataclysmic rate, the removal, blockage and/or inaccessibility of tangible items of our precious American Christian heritage. The latter boldly proclaims the hand of God in the affairs of this nation. The purpose and function of this History Curriculum is therefore to take you by the hand through ten fascinating lessons at the seat of government. We will study America's rich Christian foundations through the art, architecture, sculpture and inscriptions of its landmarks, in concert with the original historic documents of *this nation under God*.

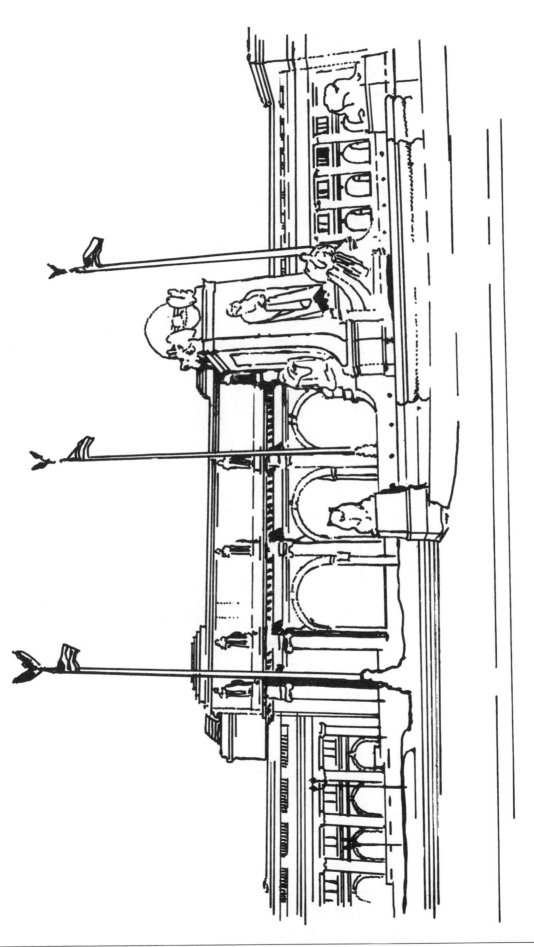

Union Station and The Christopher Columbus Memorial Fountain.

The Christopher Columbus Memorial Fountain, 1912
by Lorado Taft & Daniel H. Burnham,
in front of Union Station.

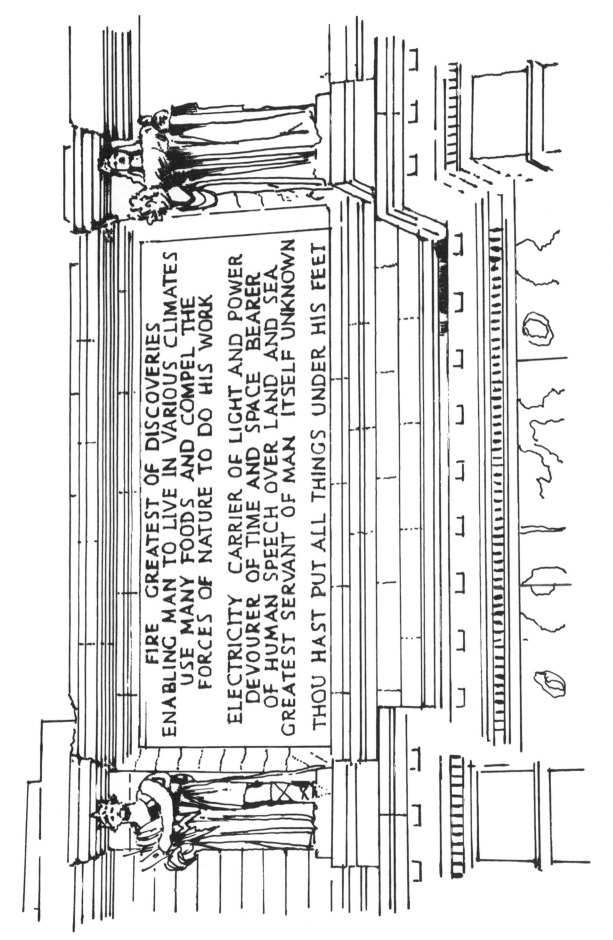

Front facade of Union Station – "Thou Hast Put All Things Under His Feet." Psalm 8:6.

FIRE GREATEST OF DISCOVERIES
ENABLING MAN TO LIVE IN VARIOUS CLIMATES
USE MANY FOODS AND COMPEL THE
FORCES OF NATURE TO DO HIS WORK

ELECTRICITY CARRIER OF LIGHT AND POWER
DEVOURER OF TIME AND SPACE BEARER
OF HUMAN SPEECH OVER LAND AND SEA
GREATEST SERVANT OF MAN ITSELF UNKNOWN

THOU HAST PUT ALL THINGS UNDER HIS FEET

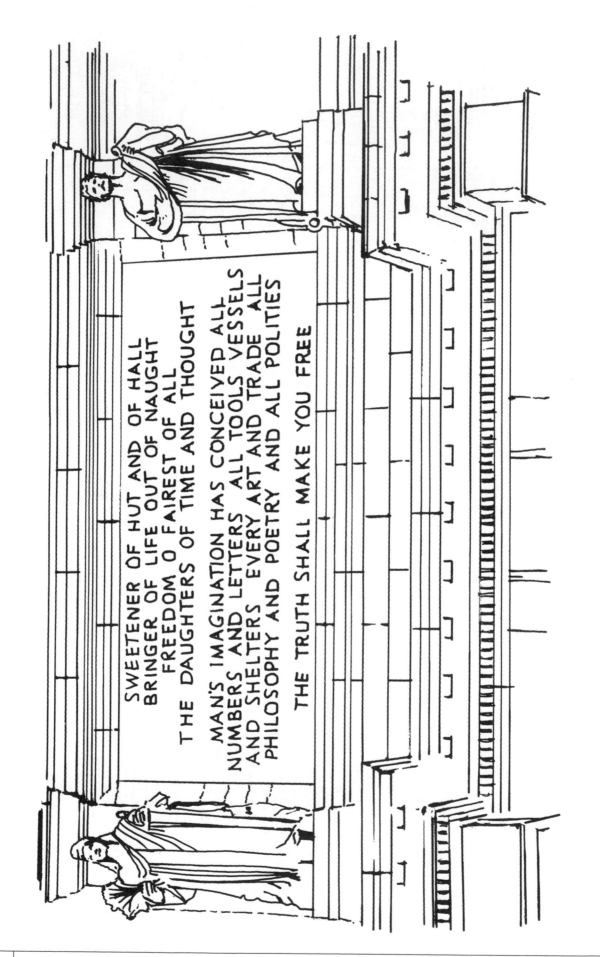

SWEETENER OF HUT AND OF HALL
BRINGER OF LIFE OUT OF NAUGHT
FREEDOM O FAIREST OF ALL
THE DAUGHTERS OF TIME AND THOUGHT

MAN'S IMAGINATION HAS CONCEIVED ALL
NUMBERS AND LETTERS ALL TOOLS VESSELS
AND SHELTERS EVERY ART AND TRADE ALL
PHILOSOPHY AND POETRY AND ALL POLITIES

THE TRUTH SHALL MAKE YOU FREE

Front facade of Union Station – "The Truth Shall Make You Free" John 8:32.

The Christian Heritage Of Our Nation - History Curriculum

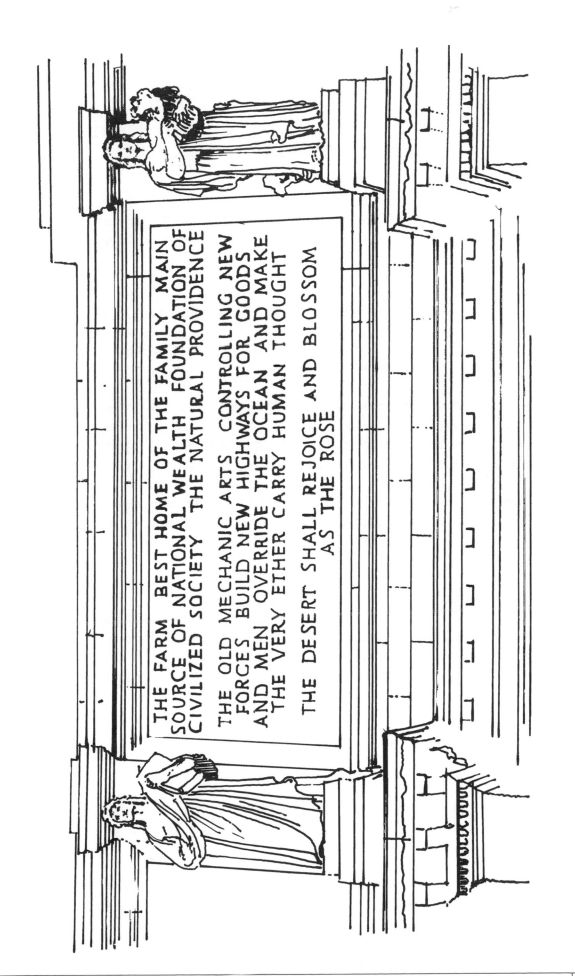

THE FARM BEST HOME OF THE FAMILY MAIN
SOURCE OF NATIONAL WEALTH FOUNDATION OF
CIVILIZED SOCIETY THE NATURAL PROVIDENCE

THE OLD MECHANIC ARTS CONTROLLING NEW
FORCES BUILD NEW HIGHWAYS FOR GOODS
AND MEN OVERRIDE THE OCEAN AND MAKE
THE VERY ETHER CARRY HUMAN THOUGHT

THE DESERT SHALL REJOICE AND BLOSSOM
AS THE ROSE

Front facade of Union Station – "The Desert shall Rejoice and Blossom as the Rose" Isaiah 35:1.

LESSON 1

UNION STATION AND THE CHRISTOPHER COLUMBUS MEMORIAL FOUNTAIN

Towards the middle of the nineteenth century, the advent of the locomotive brought about a new way of life. An 1896 article written by former stagecoach driver, Charles Eliot, appeared in the *Washington Evening Star*. It describes a quaint, but outmoded means of travel:

> Every night after supper at the taverns where we stopped, they would have a royal good time. A royal blue time, they called it, for you see, they knowed nothing about painting the town red. So they came on until they got to Fredericksburg (Va.), where they cleaned themselves up, took a bath, and come into Washington, fresh as kids.[4]

In 1903, Congress passed an Act "to provide for a union railroad in the District of Columbia and for other purposes." Architect Daniel H. Burnham, who headed the 1892 World Columbian Exhibition in Chicago, was chosen as designer and architect of Union Station, completed in 1908. The six statues on the front facade of this elegant white marble edifice are the work of Louis Saint-Gaudens, son of renowned American sculptor, Augustus Saint-Gaudens.[5] Each 18-foot tall granite statue weighs twenty-five tons.[6] Noble ideals confront the traveller, as he catches sight of the carefully-chosen inscriptions depicting each silhouetted figure. Charles W. Eliot, former President of Harvard University, was consulted in choosing a theme for both sculpture and inscription. Beneath the statue for "Fire and Electricity," God's words through David, King of Israel, ring true: "Thou hast put all things under his feet."[7] This quotation comes from Psalm Eight, which reflects God's glory and man's dignity. Under the statue "Freedom and Imagination," Christ's message from John 8:32 is cited: "The Truth shall Make you Free." Jesus is here referring to abiding in His Words. Beneath the inscription for "Agriculture and Mechanics," the Old Testament prophetic utterance pertaining to Israel is given: "The desert shall rejoice and blossom as the rose." (Isaiah 35:1)[8]

Inscribed on the attic wall of the State Entrance, South Elevation, are beautiful and timely words of exhortation to all who pass by:

> Let all the Ends thou Aim'st at be Thy Country's, Thy God's and Truth's, Be Noble, and the Nobleness that lies in other men, sleeping but never dead, will rise in majesty to meet thine own.

Union Station is one of the most attractive and interesting sights in the nation's capital. The Columbus Fountain enhances its driveway with a fifteen-foot tall statue of Italian-born traveler and discoverer of the new world, Christopher Columbus. Three handsome flagpoles tower above his fountain, symbolizing Columbus' three sailing ships—the "Nina," the "Pinta" and the "Santa Maria." To the right, the Old World, with its teeming population and limited horizons is portrayed in the form of a wizened old man. The New World, with its wide open spaces and innovative ideas is seen in the figure of a young and forward-looking American Indian, to the left.

Not many people are aware of Christopher Columbus' deep faith in God and His Son, Jesus Christ. Furthermore, very few people realize that it was this faith which was the impetus that initiated his whole voyage. Columbus wrote a book entitled *Book of Prophecies*, in which he copied down Scripture pertaining to bringing the gospel to unknown coastlands. The book was only recently translated into English from the original Latin and Spanish versions by a great scholar, Dr. August Kling. It was my privilege to spend several fascinating hours sharing research finds with Dr. Kling prior to his death in 1986.

Columbus' entire voyage was funded and made possible through Queen Isabel and King Ferdinand of Spain— uniquely in light of its missionary outreach. Isabel herself having a strong Christian commitment, the populace accepted and embraced Columbus' tenuous expedition primarily for evangelistic reasons.

His real name, early history books disclose, was Cristobal Colon. His writings show a strong thread of Christianity. Even his signature is encased in a triangular pattern, with the beautiful names of Almighty God—El Shaddai (Almighty God); Adonai (Lord God) abbreviated, written above his signature, Christopher Ferens (Christ Bearer):

"X.p.o. Ferens," was meant to represent Columbus as the cross-bearer or the Christ-bearer:

When the expedition found its first nugget of gold, it was carefully wrapped and sent back to Columbus' son, Don Diego, to deliver to Queen Isabel. It included detailed instructions in writing, telling him "to return it to her so that she may see the miracle of the Lord and remember to whom she ought to thank for it."

Six years after Columbus' discovery of the New World we see that the spiritual welfare of the native people was still of primary importance to him. In his famous mayorazgo (Testament of Founding Hereditary Family Estate), dated Thursday, 22nd February, 1498, he states:

Also I order to said Don Diego, my son, or to him who will inherit said mayorazgo, that he shall help to maintain and sustain on the Island Espanola four good teachers of the holy theology with the intention to convert to our holy religion all those people in the Indias, and when it pleases God that the income of the mayorazgo will increase, that then also be increased the number of such devoted persons who will help all these people to become Christians. And may he not worry about the money that it will be necessary to spend for the purpose. . .[9]

Through the ages of history, many great inventors, scientists and visionaries have acknowledged the Bible and the leading of the Holy Spirit as the basis for their contributions which revolutionized the world of their day. Columbus was no exception. The following lengthy quotation from the Introduction of Christopher Columbus' *Book of Prophecies*, summarizes not only his deep commitment to the gospel mandate, but also points to the Bible as the very source of his inspiration:

At a very early age I began to sail upon the ocean. For more than forty years, I have sailed everywhere that people go. I prayed to the most merciful Lord about my heart's great desire, and He gave me the spirit and the intelligence for the task: seafaring, astronomy, geometry, arithmetic, skill in drafting spherical maps and placing correctly the cities, rivers, mountains and ports. I also studied cosmology, history, chronology and philosophy.

It was the Lord who put into my mind (I could feel His hand upon me) the fact that it would be possible to sail from here to the Indies. All who heard of my project rejected it with laughter, ridiculing me. There is no question that the inspiration was from the Holy Spirit, because he comforted me with rays of marvelous illumination from the Holy Scriptures, a strong and clear testimony from the 44 books of the Old Testament, from the four Gospels, and from the 23 Epistles of the blessed Apostles, encouraging me continually to press forward, and without ceasing for a moment they now encourage me to make haste.

Our Lord Jesus desired to perform a very obvious miracle in the voyage to the Indies, to comfort me and the whole people of God. I spent seven years in the royal court, discussing the matter with many persons of great reputation and wisdom in all the arts; and in the end they concluded that it was all foolishness, so they gave it up. But since things generally came to pass that were predicted by our Savior Jesus Christ, we should also believe that this particular prophecy will come to pass. In support of this, I offer the gospel text, Matthew 24:35, in which Jesus said that all things would pass away, but not his marvelous Word. He also affirmed that it was necessary that all things be fulfilled that were prophesied by Himself and by the prophets.

I said that I would state my reasons. I hold alone to the sacred and Holy Scriptures, and to the interpretations of prophecy given by certain devout persons.

It is possible that those who see this book will accuse me of being unlearned in literature, of being a layman and a sailor. I reply with the words of Matthew

11: 25: "Lord, because thou hast hid these things from the wise and prudent, and hath revealed them unto babes."

The Holy Scripture testifies in the Old Testament by our Redeemer Jesus Christ, that the world must come to an end. The signs of when this must happen are given by Matthew, Mark and Luke. The prophets also predicted many things about it.

Our Redeemer Jesus Christ said that before the end of the world, all things must come to pass that had been written by the prophets. The prophets wrote in various ways. Isaiah is the one most praised by Jerome, Augustine and by the other theologians. They all say that Isaiah was not only a prophet, but an evangelist as well. Isaiah goes into great detail in describing future events and in calling all people to our holy catholic faith.

Most of the prophecies of Holy Scripture have been fulfilled already. I am a most unworthy sinner, but I have cried out to the Lord for grace and mercy; and they have covered me completely. I have found the sweetest consolations since I made it my whole purpose to enjoy His marvelous presence.

For the execution of the journey to the Indies I did not make use of intelligence, mathematics or maps. It is simply the fulfillment of what Isaiah had prophesied. All this is what I desire to write down for you in this book.

No one should fear to undertake any task in the name of our Savior, if it is just and if the intention is purely for His holy service. The working out of all things has been assigned to each person by our Lord, but it all happens according to His sovereign will, even though He gives advice. He lacks nothing that it is in the power of man to give Him. Oh what a gracious Lord, who desires that people should perform for Him things for which He holds Himself responsible! Day and night, moment by moment, everyone should express to Him their most devoted gratitude.

I said that some of the prophecies remained yet to be fulfilled. These are great and wonderful things for the earth and the signs are that the Lord is hastening the end. The fact that the gospel must still be preached to so many lands in such a short time—this is what convinces me.[10]

Columbus' Burden for Lost Souls

Columbus' letter to Lord Raphael Sansix, dated May 3, 1493 is entitled, *Concerning the Islands Lately Discovered*, and gives insight, once again, into the soul of this great American hero, his intense love of the Lord, his life of prayer, and his desire to bring the life-saving gospel of Jesus Christ to these distant shores. It is hereunder excerpted:

> . . .But great and wonderful is this thing, neither attributable to our merits, but to the holy Christian Faith, and to the piety and religion of our sovereigns: because what the human understanding was unable to attain, that thing the

Divine understanding granted to human creatures. For God is accustomed to hearken to His servants, and those who love His precepts, even to the accomplishment of impossibilities, as it hath befallen us in the present case, who have accomplished those things, which hitherto the strength of mortals hath not attained. For if others have written or spoken anything of these Islands, all have done so by quibbles or conjectures, no one affirms that he has seen them. Whence the whole matter seemed almost a fable.

Let, therefore, the King and Queen, our Sovereigns, and their most happy Realms; together with all Christian regions,—let us all give thanks to our Lord Jesus Christ the Saviour, who hath bestowed on us so great a triumph . . . Let Christ exult on earth, as He exults in Heaven, foreseeing as He does, that so many souls of people heretofore lost, are now about to be saved. Let us also rejoice, both by reason of the exultation of our faith, and by reason of the increase of our temporal things, of which things not only Spain but all Christendom will be partakers. These things, as they have been promptly achieved, so are they briefly related . . .[11]

Hardships at Sea

There were many hardships and difficulties on his four expeditions to the new world, especially in the latter trips, such as storms at sea, ships worm-eaten and not able to stay afloat, and mutinies.

God's Timely Help in the Midst of Tribulation

Perhaps one of Columbus' most insightful and moving letters was the one he wrote from Jamaica on July 7, 1503 during his last voyage to America. It depicts his inner soul, his human frailty in perilous times, and God's timely help in the midst of tribulation. It is here excerpted:

In January the mouth of the river had closed. In April the ships were all worm-eaten and would not stay afloat. The river now formed a canal through which we drew three of them, empty, with great difficulty. The boats were sent in again for salt and water; the sea rose and became turbulent, which prevented their coming out. The Indians were many in number and began a battle which ended in slaughter. My brother and the other people were all in a ship that remained inside. I was outside, all alone, on that wild coast, with a high fever and utterly exhausted. All hope of escape had left me; I worked myself to the highest part of the ship, and with sobs and in tremulous tones called for help upon the war-captains of your Highnesses, in every direction, but never an answer did I get. Worn out, I fell asleep groaning. A voice full of pity I heard saying: "Oh, fool that thou art and slow to believe in and serve thy God, the Lord of all! What more did He do for Moses or for David His servant? Since the day of thy birth hath He ever watched over thee. When thou didst reach an age that seemed well to Him, marvelously He made thy name resound throughout the earth. The Indies, that are so rich a part of the world, He hath given thee for thine own. Thou didst distribute them as it pleased thee, and He gave thee power to do so. To the barriers of the seas that were closed with such mighty chains, hath He given thee the keys; and thou wast obeyed in so many lands and didst receive such just fame among Christians. What more did He do for the people of Israel when He took them out of Egypt? Or for David, who, from a shepherd He made King of Judea? Turn to Him, and see thine error. His mercy is infinite;. . .vast and many are the gifts that He can bestow. Abraham was more than one hundred years old when he begat Isaac; and Sarah, was she a young girl? Thou callest for uncertain help—answer; who has afflicted thee so greatly and so often, God, or the world? The privileges bestowed by the Lord are never taken away and His promises are never broken;. . .His every promise is faithfully kept and fulfilled in overflowing measure. . .I have told thee what thy Creator hath done for thee, and what He doth for all of His children: now behold the reward that hath been thine for the dangers and hardships that thou hast suffered while serving others!" Thus in a dazed state did I listen; but I could make no answer to words so true except to weep for my errors. The speaker, whoever he might be, closed by saying: "Fear not; have faith; all thy tribulations are written upon marble, and not without cause. . ."[12]

Columbus' Primary Goal in Life

The above shows a humble man who knew God, and whose purpose in life was to serve Him. What a rich Christian heritage can be traced to the year of our Lord 1492, when Christopher Columbus, "Christ-bearer to the Unchartered Isles," brought the gospel of Jesus Christ to America.

LESSON ONE

Union Station and the Christopher Columbus Memorial Fountain

I. Suggestions for Study

    a)   Read the Lesson material carefully.

    b)   Look up Spain; Espanola; San Salvador, El Salvador; and Jamaica on your world map at home.

II. Lesson Material

Text: Lesson 1 - Union Station and the Christopher Columbus Memorial Fountain.

III. 1. The kind of man Christopher Columbus was:

    i)   Who did Christopher Columbus say had "put in his mind" and "gave him the spirit and intelligence for the task" of sailing from Spain to America? (Circle one)

        a)   His father
        b)   Pope Alexander VI
        c)   The Lord
        d)   Queen Isabel of Spain

    ii)   What did Christopher Columbus not employ in his journey to the Indies? (Circle correct answers)

        a)   mathematics
        b)   maps
        c)   intelligence
        d)   illumination of the Holy Spirit

    iii)   Christopher Columbus' primary reason for making his voyage to the unknown West was: (Circle one)

        a)   to discover gold and rich spices
        b)   to find a short route to the Indies
        c)   to trade with the Indians
        d)   to bring the Gospel

iv)   Christopher Columbus was: (Circle correct answers)

    a)   an explorer
    b)   a map-maker
    c)   a Christian
    d)   a tent-maker
    e)   a printer

v)   In making his voyage to the unknown West, Christopher Columbus relied upon: (Circle one)

    a)   his intelligence
    b)   mathematics
    c)   the winds
    d)   Scripture
    e)   maps

vi)   After discovering the first nugget of gold, Christopher Columbus: (Circle one)

    a)   kept it for himself
    b)   sold it
    c)   buried it
    d)   sent it to his family in Spain
    e)   gave it to Queen Isabel, telling her to thank the Lord for it

vii)   Christopher Columbus signed his letters as follows: (Circle one)

    a)   His Excellency
    b)   His exalted Highness
    c)   Christ-bearer
    d)   the High Admiral
    e)   His majesty

viii)   Christopher Columbus wrote that it was: (Circle one)

    a)   his father
    b)   his son
    c)   the Holy Spirit
    d)   Marco Polo

who had inspired him to make his journey to the unknown West.

2. Christian character traits:

Select 10 Christian virtues, values and morals of this great American hero from the selected texts of original writings and letters of Christopher Columbus. List them below:

a. _____ f. _____

b. _____ g. _____

c. _____ h. _____

d. _____ i. _____

e. _____ j. _____

IV. Illustrate your work with pictures, outline map, models and drawings.

V. Memory Verse: Christopher Columbus' Scripture verse kept him faithful to God's call upon his life, "to bring the Gospel to Unknown Coastlands."

And I will set a sign among them and will send survivors from them to the nations: Tarshish, Put, Lud, Meshesh, Rosh, Tubal and Javan, to the distant coastlands that have neither heard My fame nor seen My glory. And they will declare my glory among the nations.

Isaiah 66:19

East Steps – U.S. Capitol.

"The Genius of America" – Triangular Pediment above the Main East Steps of the U.S. Capitol.

The Christian Heritage Of Our Nation - History Curriculum

The Christopher Columbus Bronze Doorway,
by Randolph Rogers – U.S. Capitol – Main, East Entrance.

The Christopher Columbus Bronze Doorway. Christopher Columbus leaving the Convent of La Rabida, Spain. Don Perez, Queen Isabel's confessor, gives him a Letter of Introduction to the Queen, who funded the entire voyage. (Second panel from the bottom, left hand side.)

The Christian Heritage Of Our Nation - History Curriculum

After the frieze "Landing of Columbus, 1492" by Constantino Brumidi. Circular painting within the inner dome of the Main Rotunda, U.S. Capitol.

Taken from "Signing of the Declaration of Independence, Independence Hall, Philadelphia, July 4th, 1776" by John Trumbull.

The Christian Heritage Of Our Nation - History Curriculum

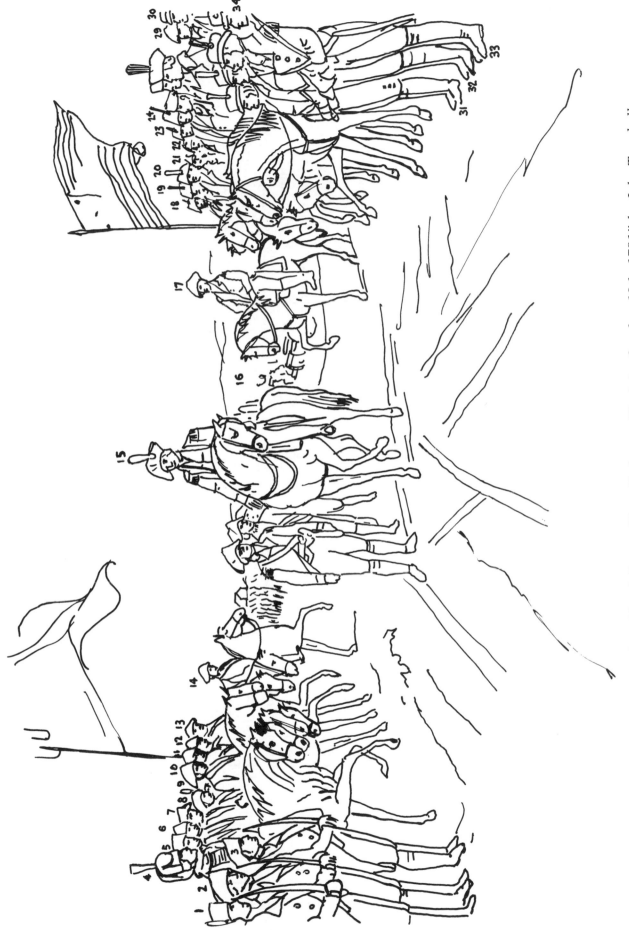

After the painting, "Surrender of Lord Cornwallis at Yorktown, Virginia, October 19th, 1781" by John Trumbull.

Surrender of Lord Cornwallis at Yorktown, Va. October 19th 1781.

The portraits of the French Officers were obtained in Paris 1787 and painted by Trumbull from the living draft in the house of Mr. Jefferson, then Minister to France from the United States.

1. Count Deuxpoints
   Colonel of French Infantry
2. Duke de Laval Montmorency
   Colonel of French Infantry
3. Count Custine
   Colonel of French Infantry
4. Duke de Lauzun
   Colonel of French Cavalry
5. General Choizy
6. Viscount Viomenil
7. Marquis de St. Simon
8. Count Fersen
   Aide-de-camp of Count Rochambeau
9. Count Charles Damas
   Aide-de-camp of Count Rochambeau
10. Marquis Chastellux
11. Baron Viomenil
12. Count de Barras, Admiral
13. Count de Grasse, Admiral
14. Count Rochambeau
    General en Chef des Francais
15. General Lincoln
16. E. Stevens
    Colonel of American Artillery
17. General Washington
    Commander in Chief
18. Thomas Nelson
    Governor of Virginia
19. Marquis de Lafayette
20. Baron Steuben

21. Colonel Cobb
    Aide-de-camp to General Washington
22. Colonel Trumbull
    Secretary to General Washington
23. Maj. Gen. James Clinton, New York
24. General Gist, Maryland
25. Gen. Anthony Wayne, Pennsylvania
26. General Hand, Pennsylvania
    Adjutant General
27. Gen. Peter Muhlenberg,
    Pennsylvania
28. Maj. Gen. Henry Knox
    Commander of Artillery
29. Lieut. Col. E. Huntington
    Acting Aide-de-camp of General
    Lincoln
30. Col. Timothy Pickering
    Quartermaster General
31. Col. Alexander Hamilton
    commanding Light Infantry
32. Col. John Laurens, South Carolina
33. Col. Walter Stuart, Philadelphia
34. Col. Nicholas Fish, New York

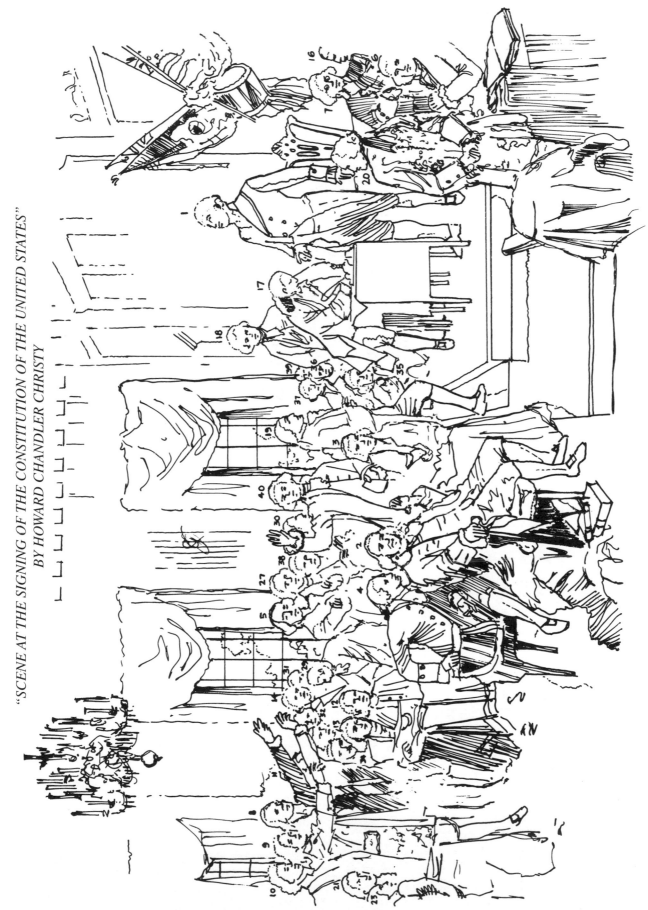

"SCENE AT THE SIGNING OF THE CONSTITUTION OF THE UNITED STATES"
BY HOWARD CHANDLER CHRISTY

Main Stairwell adjacent to the House of Representatives, U.S. Capitol.

Key: "Scene at the Signing of the Constitution of the United States" by Howard Chandler Christy.

1. Washington, George, Va.
2. Franklin, Benjamin, Pa.
3. Madison, James, Va.
4. Hamilton, Alexander, N.Y.
5. Morris, Gouverneur, Pa.
6. Morris, Robert, Pa.
7. Wilson, James, Pa.
8. Pinckney, Chas.
     Cotesworth, S.C.
9. Pinckney, Chas, S.C.
10. Rutledge, John, S.C.
11. Butler, Pierce, S.C.
12. Sherman, Roger, Conn.
13. Johnson, William Samuel, Conn.
14. McHenry, James, Md.
15. Read, George, Del.
16. Bassett, Richard, Del.
17. Spaight, Richard Dobbs, N.C.
18. Blount, William, N.C.
19. Williamson, Hugh, N.C.
20. Jenifer, Daniel of
     St. Thomas, Md.

21. King, Rufus, Mass.
22. Gorham, Nathaniel, Mass.
23. Dayton, Jonathan, N.J.
24. Carroll, Daniel, Md.
25. Few, William, Ga.
26. Baldwin, Abraham, Ga.
27. Langdon, John, N.H.
28. Gilman, Nicholas, N.H.
29. Livingston, William, N.J.
30. Paterson, William, N.J.
31. Mifflin, Thomas, Pa.
32. Clymer, George, Pa.
33. FitzSimons, Thomas, Pa.
34. Ingersoll, Jared, Pa.
35. Bedford, Gunning, Jr., Del.
36. Brearley, David, N.J.
37. Dickinson, John, Del.
38. Blair, John, Va.
39. Broom, Jacob, Del.
40. Jackson, William, Secretary.

MOSES

Moses – facing the Speaker's Chair, U.S. House of Representatives.

"The George Washington kneeling in Prayer"
stained-glass window. Prayer Room of the U.S. Capitol.

The Christian Heritage Of Our Nation - History Curriculum

LESSON 2

THE UNITED STATES CAPITOL - LEGISLATIVE BRANCH OF OUR GOVERNMENT

A pause on the east steps of the Capitol building gives insight into the purpose for which our government was created. The triangular pediment directly above this traditional site for the inauguration of United States Presidents, depicts a scene entitled: *The Genius of America.* Armed America stands in the center with a spear behind her, and a shield bearing *U.S.A.* upon it. She gazes at Hope, to the right, who beckons to her to proceed. However, America points towards Justice, to the left, who holds a pair of scales in her left hand and a scroll in her right, reading: *Constitution, 17 September 1787.* The message conveyed here is that without justice, there is no hope for America, our justice being based upon the Constitution, which is based upon the Declaration of Independence, which in turn is based upon the justice of God's words.

The Rotunda of the Capitol, with its impressive dome, stands before us, with the House of Representatives to the left and the Senate to the right. Nineteen and a half feet tall, bronze, *Armed Freedom* stands atop the dome. The work of talented sculptor Thomas Crawford, she holds a sheathed sword in her right hand and a wreath and a shield in her left. Her flowing robes are held together with a buckle bearing the letters. *U.S.* Upon her head is a helmet encircled with thirteen stars and an eagle's head and feathers, placed there to camouflage a liberated slave's cap, original concept of the sculptor.

We enter the majestic, dome-like interior of the Rotunda through the Christopher Columbus bronze doorway, work of Randolph Rogers. Scenes and main landmarks in the life of this discoverer and explorer of the new world, whose main goal was "to propagate the gospel to unknown coastlands," are depicted upon nine panels. The Rotunda is where Presidents who die in office lie in state before the funeral procession proceeds along Pennsylvania Avenue to the White House, and then to the church of their affiliation. This circular chamber houses eight valuable oil paintings. The four paintings nearest the main entranceway indicate the godly foundations upon which our nation was established. *Landing of Columbus at the island of Guanahani, West Indies, October 12, 1492* portrays a flag with a Latin cross upon it, while a friar holds up the cross of our Lord and Savior Jesus Christ. *Embarkation of the Pilgrims at Delft Haven, Holland, July 22, 1620,* by Robert W. Weir, is a touching scene of prayer and worship to Almighty God, with bended knee and bowed head. The focal point of this scene aboard ship is an open Bible, the one true guide and source of comfort for the earliest settlers in the land. *God with Us* reads an inscription on the uppermost left-hand sail (Matthew 1:23). *Baptism of Pocahontas at Jamestown, Virginia, 1613,* by John G. Chapman, shows this Indian princess, now immortalized in early Jamestown history, kneeling demurely before a priest, as she awaits baptism into the Christian faith; and *The Discovery of the Mississippi by DeSoto in 1541*, portrays a giant cross being erected in the presence of native American Indians.

John Trumbull, who served in the Revolutionary War under George Washington, painted great landmarks of America's founding history, being present at these events. Four of his famous paintings adorn the walls of the Main Rotunda. They are: *"Signing of the Declaration of Independence, Philadelphia, July 4th, 1776;" "Surrender of General Bourgoyne at Saratoga, New York, October 17th, 1777," "Surrender of Lord Cornwallis at Yorktown, Virginia, October 19th, 1781,"* and *"General George Washington resigning his Commission to Congress as Commander in Chief of the Army at Annapolis, Maryland, December 23rd, 1783."*

Constantino Brumidi, a political refugee from Rome, envisioned and designed the three-hundred-foot frieze encircling the inner dome of the Rotunda.[13] It stands fifty-eight feet above the stone floor. This unusual masterpiece comprises four hundred years of American history. Beginning with America in History and the arrival of Christopher Columbus in 1492, each of the sixteen panels depicts an important milestone in the making of the nation's history. Lying upon his back on an elevated scaffolding, Brumidi leaned backwards to gain a clearer perspective of his finished work. A fall from the scaffolding left him holding onto the rung of a ladder, until he could be rescued.[14] It was thus a few months later, in the year 1880, that Brumidi, one of the Capitol's most talented artists, relinquished his life. Heart failure, resulting from the fall, caused his death. Brumidi had spent 25 years painting scenes of American history, flora and fauna. His purpose was "to make beautiful the Capitol of the one country on earth in which there is liberty."[15] This he did with deep gratitude to a nation he loved; a nation which had opened its arms wide to him in his hour of need.

His successor, Filippo Costaggini, completed the remaining eight scenes, crowding them to insert his own three historic creations.[16] The Joint Committee on the Library declined his proposition to paint them, however, leaving a blank space in the frieze until the year 1953.[17] At that time, Allyn Cox, official artist to the Capitol, completed the work with later scenes of American history.[18] They comprise the Civil War, the Spanish-American War and the first successful flight undertaken by the Wright brothers in 1903. The majestic grace of this creation, and its equally breath-taking *Apotheosis of George Washington* in the dome of the Rotunda, are an inspiration to the millions who visit the Capitol each year.

Statuary Hall

Statuary Hall displays 44 statues of great men and women who helped fashion the life of the nation. Junipero Serra, a Franciscan friar who brought the good news of eternal life through faith in Jesus Christ to California, stands out in originality. He holds the cross of Christ in his right hand and a model mission in his left. Why the mission? San Francisco, San Carlos, San Antonio de Padua, San Diego and others, were originally missionary settlements, established with the purpose of bringing salvation to the lost. What a testimony to the creation of these West Coast cities! Not far from him stands Jason Lee, first missionary to the State of Oregon. He was a prominent minister and statesman who knew the Word of God well and applied it to his life. On the opposite side of the room stands Illinois' Frances F. Willard, founder of the World's Christian Temperance Union in 1883, and associated with Dwight Moody's Evangelistic Movement. Marcus Whitman was a great medical missionary to Washington Territory. Dressed in a pioneer outfit, his Bible under one arm, and his medical equipment in the other hand, this great man of God stood firmly upon the conviction of God's Word. He and his wife Narcissa brought many souls to the Lord, being finally massacred by the Indians in 1847.

In the Senate Connecting Corridor toward the Old Supreme Court Chamber, the statue of Dr. Crawford Williamson Long, Georgia's Tribute, is greatly to be admired. This great American hero invented the use of sulphuric ether as an anesthesia in surgery. Upon the base of the statue are inscribed his own words:

My profession is to me a ministry from God.

A handsome bronze plaque on the adjoining East wall of the Small Senate Rotunda was erected on the centennial anniversary of a famous event. It honors Samuel F.B. Morse, inventor of the telegraph. He wired the first telegraph message *What Hath God Wrought!* (Numbers 23:23) from the Capitol to Baltimore on May 24, 1844.

The House of Representatives

Above the Speaker's Chair in the House of Representatives, an inscription states in whom we place our trust. "In God We Trust," it confidently asserts. On either side of the Speaker's Chair, two life-size portraits catch the viewer's eye. They represent George Washington and the Marquis de Lafayette. Washington's position of prominence is assured because of the fact that he was the instrument whom God chose to found the United States of America. But what about the portrait of Lafayette? How did it find its place on the left-hand-side of the Speaker's Chair? This hero of the American Revolution gained entrance by virtue of the fact that he was the first foreigner to address a Joint Session of Congress.[19] The event took place at the time of the Marquis' triumphal return to America in 1824, when he addressed an assembled Congress in what is now called Statuary Hall.[20] A glance at the walls of this crucial center for decision-making discloses bas-relief profiles of famous lawmakers of the past. Is it by sheer coincidence, or by Divine intervention, that the only full face, the head of Moses, to whom Almighty God gave the Ten Commandments, stands out directly opposite the Speaker's Chair—a silent reminder to all who enter of the awesome responsibility placed upon the leaders of the *One nation under God.*

Voting within the House of Representatives takes place by means of red, green and yellow buttons behind the delegates' chairs. A swift tally of votes appears upon a plexiglass electronic board above the Reporters' Gallery. The blue damask facade, perfect counterfeit of the remaining wall coverings, lights up and reveals an electronic device of modern-day ingenuity. All 435 delegates are represented with "yea," "nay" or "abstain" signs next to their names. One sits enraptured by the quiet beauty and efficiency of this room where so much power is wielded, and where binding national policies are made.

The Senate

The United States Senate is composed of one hundred Senators, two representing each of the fifty states in the Union. Each elected officer serves a six-year term, on a renewable basis. The Vice President of the United States presides over the Senate. The business of the Senate is generally done by a president pro tempore, however.

Encircling the inner walls are marble busts of twenty Vice Presidents of the United States, all of whom served as President of the Senate. [21]

The Prayer Room

A small private room in the Capitol building serves as a quiet place of prayer and meditation for Senators and Congressmen who wish to turn their thoughts and minds to spiritual things. The room was completed and opened for use in March of 1955. From various members of the Senate and House of Representatives come the following quotations:

> . . . a place at the Capitol where we might meditate and pray, where the mood of prayer could be encouraged. [22]

> We legislators might insist that in no other area are men driven so powerfully as in our profession. How well we do our job in creativeness must be left to the judgment of our contemporaries and of history. But as creatures seeking peace of mind, we should use the facilities of meditation and prayer with assurance that we will not be misjudged, that we will be permitted this aid to moral exercise, and that our private devotions will be respected . . . [23]

> One of the finest things that this Congress has done, one of the finest things that any Congress has done, or could do. . . [24]

To date, no less than 13 members of Congress, have celebrated their marriages in this beautiful setting. [25] A focal point in the room is a handsome stained-glass window, known as the Prayer Window. An oval-shaped central design encloses the figure of George Washington, with hands clasped in prayer. Above the kneeling figure, "This Nation under God" stands out in capital letters. Encircling the symbol of communion with God, are the opening words of Psalm 16:

> Preserve me, O God, for in Thee do I put my trust.

An outer, arch-shaped frame contains the names of our 50 states in the Union. Beneath the figure lost in prayer, the seal of the United States stands out, on the one hand depicting prominence and success, and on the other, subjection to its God and King.

Officially Recorded Presidential Inaugural Scriptures Chosen by U.S. Presidents

Every four years, a U.S. President is sworn into office with his left hand upon the Bible. The traditional site for the swearing-in is the East Steps of the U.S. Capitol. Our first president, **George Washington**, however, was sworn into office in Federal Hall, New York. This took place on April 30, 1789, prior to the completion of the Capitol building. The Bible upon which the first President of the United States swore allegiance to the U.S. Constitution was published in London in 1767 by Mark Baskett. This King James Version of Holy Scripture is handsomely illustrated with biblical scenes. After taking the oath of office, Washington kissed the Bible, which had been opened at random to Genesis, Chapters 49-50, due to haste. The page of the Bible which Washington kissed is indicated by the leaf being turned down.

Verses 22-25c, excerpted from Genesis 49, read as follows:

> Joseph is a fruitful bough, even a fruitful bough by a well; whose branches run over the wall: The archers have sorely grieved him and shot at him, and hated him; But his bow abode in strength, and the arms of his hands were made strong by the hands of the mighty God of Jacob (from thence is the Shepherd, the Stone of Israel); Even by the God of thy father, who shall help thee; and by the Almighty, who shall bless thee with blessings of heaven above. . .

On March 4th, 1865, **Abraham Lincoln** was sworn into office for a second term as President of the United States. *The New York Times* describes the ceremony as follows:

> The oath to protect and maintain the Constitution of the United States was administered to Mr. Lincoln by Chief Justice Chase, in the presence of thousands, who witnessed the interesting ceremony while standing in mud almost knee-deep. *The New York Times*, New York, Sunday, March 5, 1865.

In his inaugural address which immediately followed the oath-taking, the 16th President of the United States incorporated biblical quotations from Matthew 7:1 and 18:7 respectively:

> ". . .But let us judge not that we not be judged. . ." and ". . .Woe unto the world because of its offenses, for it must needs be that offenses come, but woe to that man by whom the offense cometh."

Lincoln's only known inaugural Bible is a King James Version of the Holy Bible, published by the Oxford University Press in London. Written on its flyleaf are the following words:

> To Mrs. Sally Carroll from her devoted husband Wm. Thos. Carroll 4 March 1861

Immediately following President Lincoln's death, **Andrew Johnson** was sworn into office at the Kirkwood Hotel on April 14, 1865. His inaugural Bible is the King James Version, published by C. J. Clay, at the University Press, London.

Inscribed on the front inside board of the Bible are the words:

> Andrew Johnson's Inaugural Bible. When oath was taken his hand rested on Chapter 20 and 21 of Proverbs. The king's heart is in the hand of the Lord, as the rivers of water; he turneth it whithersoever he will. Every way of a man is right in his own eyes: But the Lord pondereth the hearts. To do justice and judgment is more acceptable to the Lord than sacrifice. Proverbs 21:1-3

Ulysses S. Grant was sworn into office for the second time on March 4, 1873. On the second blank leaf of his Inaugural Bible is inscribed:

> To Miss Nellie Grant from D. W. Middleton Clerk Sup. Ct. U.S. used for the administration of the oath, on the Second Inauguration of General U.S. Grant, as President of the United States, March 4, 1873.

The Bible was opened at the beautiful Messianic prophecy of Isaiah, which reads:

> And there shall come forth a rod out of the stem of Jesse, and a Branch shall grow out of his roots: And the Spirit of the Lord shall rest upon Him, the Spirit of wisdom and understanding, the Spirit of counsel and might, the Spirit of knowledge and the fear of the Lord; Isaiah 11:1-2

The General is purported to have been pleased with this coincidence, as he was the son of Jesse.

On the 5th of March, 1877, **Rutherford B. Hayes** was sworn into office as the nineteenth President of the United States. The Bible upon which he took the oath of office was a King James version, printed in London by George E. Eyre and William Spottiswoode, printers to the Queen's most Excellent Majesty. A single electoral vote won this difficult election for Hayes. Due to the closeness of the election, Psalm 118:11-13 might have been chosen as the Inaugural Scripture:

> They compassed me about; yea, they compassed me about: but in the name of the Lord I will destroy them. They compassed me about like bees; they are quenched as the fire of thorns: for in the name of the Lord I will destroy them. Thou hast thrust sore at me that I might fall: but the Lord helped me. Psalm 118:11-13

The Christian Heritage Of Our Nation - History Curriculum

Inscribed upon the second front blank leaf are these words:

> To Mrs. Hayes with the Compliments of D. W. Middleton Clerk Sup: Court
> U. S. Used for the administration of the oath on the Inauguration of Rutherford
> B. Hayes as President of the United States. 5th March 1877.

Below, in pencil is the notation:

> See: 118 Psalm 11 verse etc.
>   Psalm 101

James A. Garfield swore allegiance to the Constitution of the United States on March 4, 1881. His Inaugural Bible is the King James Version, S.S. Teacher's Edition, printed at the University Press, Oxford. A Certification on the second front blank leaf reads:

> Bible used at the Inauguration of James A. Garfield 20th President of the United States 4th March, A.D. 1881. James H. McKenney Clerk Supreme Court U.S. (L.S.) To Mrs. J. A. Garfield with compliments James H. McKenney.

The left margin holds the following hand-written comment:

See Proverbs XXI

To the left of Proverbs 21, the following notation appears in the same hand:

> verse 1, chapter 21 kissed by President Garfield when taking oath of office.

The verse referred to reads:

> The king's heart is in the hand of the Lord, as rivers of water: He turneth it whithersoever he will. Proverbs 21:1

Chester Arthur was sworn into office privately in New York City after the death of President Garfield on September 20, 1881, and a second time in Washington, D.C. on September 22 of the same year. His Inaugural Bible is a King James Version, published by George E. Eyre and William Spottiswoode of London. A statement by the Clerk of the Supreme Court appears near the front:

> Upon this Bible the Chief Justice administered the oath of office to Chester A. Arthur 21st President of the United States. (L S.) James H. McKenney Clerk of the Supreme Court of the United States.

Psalm 31:1-2, the Scripture chosen by the President for his inauguration, is marked in pencil:

In thee, O Lord, do I put my trust; let me never be ashamed: deliver me in thy righteousness. Bow down thine ear to me; deliver me speedily: be thou my strong rock, for a house of defense to save me. Psalm 31:1-2.

Grover Cleveland's Inaugural Bible was published by the American Bible Society in 1851. He was the only President to hold office for two non-consecutive terms. In the front of the Bible is inscribed:

S.G. Cleveland from his affectionate mother July, 1852.

On the next page is inscribed:

On this Bible the oath of Office was administered to Grover Cleveland 22nd President of the United States by Hon. Morrison R. Waite, Chief Justice of the United States, March 4, 1885, Test: James H. McKenney (L.S.) Clerk Supreme Court of the United States.

The Bible upon which Cleveland took his oath of office was a small, well-worn Morocco-covered, gilt-edged Bible. It was a gift from the President's mother, when, as a youth, he first left home to seek his fortune. An interesting article by Alexander R. George entitled "Inaugural Pageant" gives us a vivid description of the first Cleveland Inauguration:

Cheers 'like the roaring of Niagara' greeted President elect Cleveland as he rode from the White House to the Capitol in an open barouche drawn by President Arthur's spanking bays. The presidential carriage was lined with black and white robes. Vice-President elect Hendricks rode in another open barouche, lined with crimson satin and pulled by four white horses, two famous Arabians in the lead. After taking the oath of office President Cleveland kissed the small, worn Bible his mother had given him as a boy when he left home. Phil Sheridan, still vigorous and ruddy, stood nearby. The 'cameramen' hurriedly spread black mantles over their machines and 'shot' the scene while hundreds of men and boys looked on from the roof of the Capitol. It was estimated there were 150,000 people massed on the grounds and nearby streets. . .

G. Hazelton, in his book entitled, *The National Capitol* writes:

By the President's special request, it (his Bible) was used for the ceremony. It was opened by the Chief Justice without any intention of selecting a particular place and the place that was kissed by the President was, therefore, the result purely of chance. As the type used in the Bible is small, the lips of the President touched six verses of 112th Psalm, from verse 5 to 10 inclusive. . . "A good man showeth favor, and lendeth: he will guide his affairs with discretion; surely he shall not be moved forever; the righteous shall be in everlasting remembrance. He shall not be afraid of evil tidings: his heart is fixed, trusting the Lord. His heart is established; he shall not be afraid, until he sees his desire upon his enemies. He hath dispersed, he hath given to the poor; his righteousness endureth forever; his horn shall be exalted with honor. The wicked shall see it, and be grieved; he shall gnash with his teeth, and melt away; the desire of the wicked shall perish." Psalm 112: 5-10

At his second inauguration in 1893, Cleveland's hand rested upon Psalm 91:12-16:

> They shall bear thee up in their hands, lest thou dash thy foot against a stone. Thou shalt tread upon the lion and adder: The young lion and the dragon shalt thou trample under feet. Because he hath set his love upon me, therefore will I deliver him: I will set him on high, because he hath known my name. He shall call upon me, and I will answer him: I will be with him in trouble; I will deliver him and honor him. With long life will I satisfy him, and show him my salvation. Psalm 91:12-16

Benjamin Harrison was inaugurated into office as President of the United States on March 4, 1889. His inaugural Bible is the S.S. Teacher's Edition of the King James Version published by the Oxford University Press. An official inscription on the first blank leaf of his Bible reads:

> I certify that this Bible was used in the administration of the oath of office on the fourth day of March, A.D. 1889, to Benjamin Harrison, the twenty-third President of the United States. Melville W. Fuller James H. McKenney, Clerk of the Supreme Court of the United States. To Mrs. Benjamin Harrison with the compliments of the Clerk.

The following lines are from Psalm 121, verses 1-6:

> I will lift up mine eyes unto the hills, from whence cometh my help. My help cometh from the Lord, which made heaven and earth. He will not suffer thy foot to be moved: he that keepeth thee will not slumber. Behold, he that keepeth Israel shall neither slumber nor sleep. The Lord is thy keeper: the Lord is thy shade upon thy right hand. The sun shall not smite thee by day, nor the moon by night. Psalm 121:1-6

William McKinley was sworn into office on March 4, 1897. Justice Fuller's certification, without the seal, is inscribed upon the first blank leaf of McKinley's first inaugural Bible, as follows:

> I certify that this Bible was used by me in admastering the oath of office to William McKinley as President of the United States on the fourth day of March, A.D. 1897. Melville W. Fuller, Chief Justice of the United States

The President's choice of Scripture passage is then pencilled in, to read:

> II Chronicles 1:10

An article appearing in *The Washington Post* of March 5, 1897, elaborates upon this auspicious event:

Sworn on a Bishop's Bible presented to Mr. M'Kinley on behalf of African Methodist Episcopal Church. Supreme Court usually provides the Book on which President takes oath of office. II Chronicles 1:10 reads as follows:

Give me now wisdom and knowledge that I may go out and come in before this people, for whom can judge this thy people that is so great?

This is the verse in the Bible that Mr. McKinley kissed yesterday, when Chief Justice Fuller had administered to him the oath of office. It is the 10th verse of the first chapter of II Chronicles. Clerk McKenny held the sacred book which fell open at this chapter, and when the newly-made President bent forward his lips were directed to this verse, probably the most appropriate in the book.

'It is a much larger Bible than you had four years ago,' remarked Mr. Cleveland, who had stood by to Mr. McKenny. 'Yes,' replied Mr. McKenny, who had carried the large volume about for an hour or so. 'I think it has been growing all that time.' The Bible is an unusually handsome and costly copy of the Testaments, made especially for the occasion in Ohio, and presented to the new President by Bishop Arnett, of Wilberforce College, a colored institution in the Buckeye State, on behalf of the African Methodist Episcopal Church. Its covers are of blue morocco with satin linings, white satin panels and gilt edges. A gold plate in the center will be engraved with the following inscription: William McKinley, President of the United States of America. Inaugurated March 4, 1897.

On March 4, 1901, McKinley swore allegiance to the U.S. Constitution with his left hand upon his second inaugural Bible. Beneath the usual certification by Chief Justice Melville W. Fuller, a pencilled inscription reads:

Proverbs 16: 20 and 21.

This beautiful and appropriate inaugural Scripture, chosen by the President, reads as follows:

He that handleth a matter wisely shall find good: and whoso trusteth in the Lord, happy is he. The wise in heart shall be called prudent: and the sweetness of the lips increaseth learning.

Theodore Roosevelt's second inauguration took place on March 4, 1905. Below Chief Justice Fuller's signature, the President had dedicated this inaugural Bible to his son as follows:

To Theodore Roosevelt, Jr. from his father March 4, 1905.

The Clerk of the Supreme Court jotted down for posterity, James 1:22-23 as Roosevelt's choice of inaugural Scripture:

> But be ye doers of the word, and not merely hearers only, deceiving your own selves. For if any be a hearer of the word, and not a doer, he is like unto a man beholding his natural face in a glass;

William Howard Taft was the only U.S. President to later become Chief Justice of the Supreme Court of the United States. Inscribed on the third sheet of his own Bible are these lines:

> I, William Howard Taft, do solemnly swear that I will faithfully execute the office of President of the United States, and will, to the best of my ability, preserve, protect and defend the Constitution of the United States.
> Wm H Taft

> I certify that this Bible was used by me in administering the oath of office to William Howard Taft as President of the United States on the 4th day of March, Nineteen hundred and nine. Melville W. Fuller, Chief Justice of the United States (L.S.)

I Kings 3:9-11, marked and dated March 4, 1909, was the passage selected by Taft for his oath of Office:

> Give therefore thy servant an understanding heart to judge thy people, that I may discern between good and bad: for who is able to judge this thy so great a people? And the speech pleased the Lord, that Solomon had asked this thing. And God said unto him, because thou hast asked this thing, and hast not asked for thyself long life; neither hast asked riches for thyself, nor hast asked the life of thine enemies; but has asked for thyself understanding to discern judgment; . . . I Kings 3:9-11

Woodrow Wilson's inaugural Bible was first used in his swearing in as Governor of the State of New Jersey, and is dated 11 January 1911. At his first inauguration, in 1913, the passage of Scripture chosen by Wilson was Psalm 119:43-46:

> And take not the word of truth utterly out of my mouth; for I have hoped in thy judgments. So shall I keep thy law continually for ever and ever. And I will walk at liberty: for I seek thy precepts. I will speak of thy testimonies also before Kings, and will not be ashamed.

A Senate document of March 5, 1917 records President Wilson's second oath-taking in graphic detail:

> Mrs. Wilson rode at Wilson's side in the parade, both to and from the Capitol, and also sat beside him all the time he stood reviewing the parade. Both Mrs. Wilson and Mrs. Marshall, the wife of the Vice President, rode through

the parade with the President and Vice President. The fact that the grand Marshal, Major General Hugh L. Scott, Chief of Staff of the Army, stood beside the President all during the review of the parade was also an innovation. Promptly at 11 o'clock the President and his personal party came from the White House. He stepped into an open landau drawn by two mettlesome bay horses, which champed and pawed the ground fretfully. Beside him sat Mrs. Wilson, and in the same carriage were Senator Lee S. Overman of North Carolina, and Representative William W. Rucker of Missouri, Chairmen, respectively, of the Senate and House Inaugural Committees. With Vice President and Mrs. Marshall rode Senator Hoke Smith of Georgia, and Francis E. Warren of Wyoming, members of the Senate Committee. In the Senate Chamber the President was seated in front of the Vice President's desk, and the committee on arrangements occupied seats on his right and left. It was found when the President ended his solemn obligation, that he had kissed the Bible upon this passage: "The Lord is our refuge; a very present help in time of trouble." (Psalm 46:1)

As the Chief Justice came to the conclusion of the oath, which the President repeated after him, very slowly, a few words at a time, the Chief Justice paused for a pronounced period, lowered his voice, and said solemnly: "So help you God." The President slowly and solemnly repeated: "So—help—me—God. . ."

President **Warren G. Harding** was sworn into office on Washington's inaugural Bible, opened at Micah 6:8:

He hath showed thee, O man, what is good; and what doth the Lord require of thee, but to do justly, and to love mercy, and to walk humbly with thy God? Micah 6:8

Calvin Coolidge's second inauguration took place on March 4, 1925. The Bible he used was a gift from his mother when he was but a boy. The President's wife, Grace Coolidge, jotted down these lines in pencil on a blank sheet near the front of the Bible:

This is the Bible upon which the President's hand rested as he took the oath of office March 4, 1925 at Washington, D.C. G.C.

The Clerk of the Supreme Court listed John 1 as the President's choice of Scripture passage for his swearing in:

In the beginning was the Word, and the Word was with God, and the Word was God. The same was in the beginning with God. All things were made by Him; and without Him was not any thing made that was made. In Him was life; and the life was the light of men. And the light shineth in darkness; and the darkness comprehended it not. There was a man sent from God, whose name was John. The same came for a witness, to bear witness of the Light, that all men through Him might believe. He was not that Light, but was sent to bear witness of that Light. That was the true Light, which lighteth every man that cometh into the world. He was in the world, and the world was made by Him, and the world knew Him not. He came unto His own, and His own received Him not. But as many as received Him, to them gave He power to become the sons of God, even to them that believe on His name: Which were born, not of blood, nor of the will of the flesh, nor of the will of man, but of God. And the Word was made flesh, and dwelt among us, and we beheld His glory, the glory as of the only begotten of the father, full of grace and truth. (John 1:1-14)

A front page column in *The New York Times*, dated March 4, 1925, gives insight into the Presidential choice:

Coolidge will kiss Bible he first read: His grandfather's book will be open at the first Chapter of St. John. His aged father arrives. Colonel is calm and silent but does remark that President was quiet, even as a boy.

President Coolidge will kiss the Bible at the first Chapter of St. John when he takes the oath of office tomorrow. The Bible is one that belonged to his grandfather from which it is said, the President learned to read between four and five years of age. According to a friend, the Coolidges were accustomed to read the Bible daily, and as a child, Mr. Coolidge took to reading it as his first book. It appears that he frequently read it to his grandfather, who died when he was about five years of age. The section which he first read was the first chapter of St. John. It had been announced that Colonel Coolidge, the President's father, would bring the family Bible containing the births and deaths of the Coolidges, for use in the ceremonies tomorrow. This proved to be incorrect, and the Bible which is in the possession of the President is his grandfather's, which his grandfather later gave to the President. It is a book about the size of the Bible-class, Oxford edition. It is not the bulky family Bible of tradition. Colonel Coolidge, who administered the oath to his son under the kerosene lamp in his Vermont home in August, 1923, arrived late this evening to be present at the ceremonies tomorrow. He declined to make any comment on things political and did not seem to be any more aroused over the event than he was when his son established the summer White House at Plymouth. He displays no more emotion than the President, and is the same, silent stamp of sturdy citizen. (*New York Times*, March 4, 1925.)

No inaugural Bible for **Herbert C. Hoover** has as yet been found. Of the several Bibles in his possession, an American Standard Version comes with the following inscribed card:

Presented by the International Council of Religious Education representing the Educational Boards of the Protestant Christian Churches of the United States and Canada. March 4, 1929.

Proverbs 29:18 was the choice made by this President as he took the oath of office:

Where there is no vision, the people cast off restraint. But he that keepeth the law, happy is he. (Proverbs 29:18) American Standard Version

Franklin D. Roosevelt's Bible, dated 1686, is the oldest of all inaugural Bibles, and the only one written in a modern foreign language. This Biblia Hollandica (Dutch) version of Scripture was used by the President during all four inaugurations. It was opened each time to I Corinthians 13:

> If I speak with the tongues of men and of angels but do not have love, I have become a noisy gong or a clanging cymbal. And if I have the gift of prophecy, and know all mysteries and knowledge; and if I have all faith, so as to remove mountains, but do not have love, I am nothing. And if I give all my possessions to feed the poor, and if I deliver my body to be burned, but do not have love, it profits me nothing. Love is patient, love is kind, and is not jealous; love does not brag and is not arrogant, does not act unbecomingly; it does not seek its own, is not provoked, does not take into account a wrong suffered, does not rejoice in unrighteousness, but rejoices in the truth; bears all things, believes all things, hopes all things, endures all things. Love never fails; but if there are gifts of prophecy, they will be done away; if there are tongues they will cease; if there is knowledge, it will be done away. For we know in part, and we prophesy in part; but when the perfect comes, the partial will be done away. When I was a child, I used to speak as a child, think as a child, reason as a child; when I became a man, I did away with childish things. For now we see in a mirror dimly, but then face to face; now I know in part, but then I shall know fully just as I also have been fully known. But now abide faith, hope, love, these three; but the greatest of these is love. (I Corinthians 13)
>
> New American Standard Version

Harry S. Truman's Second Inaugural Bible was presented to him by the citizens of Jackson County, Missouri as a memorial to his mother. One of two volumes, this magnificent Gutenberg facsimile is a Latin Vulgate translation of Scripture, being one of two volumes. Truman has penned in ink, at the bottom of the page containing Exodus 20 (The Ten Commandments):

> I placed my left hand on this 20th Chapter of Exodus, January 20, 1949 when I took the oath of office.

> Exodus 20:1-17 reads as follows:

> Then God spoke these words, saying, I am the Lord your God, who brought you out of the land of Egypt, and out of the house of slavery. You shall have no other gods before Me. You shall not make for yourself an idol, or any likeness of what is in heaven above or on the earth beneath or in the water under the earth. You shall not worship them or serve them; for I, the Lord your God, am a jealous God, visiting the iniquity of the fathers on the children, on the third and fourth generations of those who hate Me, but showing lovingkindness to thousands, to those who love Me and keep My commandments. You shall not take the name of the Lord your God in vain, for the Lord will not leave him unpunished who takes His name in vain. Remember the sabbath day, to keep it holy. Six days you shall labor and do all your work, but the seventh day is a sabbath of the Lord your God; in it you shall not do any work, you or your

son or your daughter, your male or your female servant or your cattle or your sojourner who stays with you. For in six days the Lord made the heavens and the earth, the sea and all that is in them, and rested on the seventh day; therefore the Lord blessed the sabbath day and made it holy. Honor your father and your mother, that your days may be prolonged in the land which the Lord your God gives you. You shall not murder. You shall not commit adultery. You shall not steal. You shall not bear false witness against your neighbor. You shall not covet your neighbor's house; You shall not covet your neighbor's wife or his male servant or his female servant or his ox or his donkey or anything that belongs to your neighbor. (Exodus 20:1-17)

New American Standard Version

The New York Times elaborates upon this event in its January 20, 1949 issue:

Truman and Barkley Take Oaths in Capitol at Noon. Record Inauguration seen. President Truman asserted tonight that his supreme interest was to see the United States assume the world leadership that God has intended. He said that he would try to achieve this goal for the benefit of the people of the whole world and not for the selfish benefit of this or any other country. . . President Truman announced today that when he takes the oath of office tomorrow, his hand will rest on two Bibles, one opened at the Sermon on the Mount and the other opened at the 10 Commandments. He especially recommended the 10th Commandment for observance in the Capital city.

The Chief Executive, it became known also, has promised to turn his private papers over to his home town of Independence, Mo., for deposit in a Truman Museum to be established there. This was disclosed with the announcement that the facsimile of the Gutenberg Bible to be used tomorrow will be placed in the Independence public library until the museum is established. Reporters and photographers were in a swarm around Mr. Truman's desk while he was being photographed with the holy books when the President gave his little homily on the Commandments. Also present were members of the staff and Frank Rucker, Vice President of the Independence Examiner, a daily newspaper, and Homer Clements, Superintendent of Schools of Mr. Truman's home Jackson County.

Texts make a good program: Mr. Truman turned familiarly to the Sermon on the Mount in his plain, favorite White House Bible, and to Exodus in the Gothic Latin he could not read in the Gutenberg facsimile, a 2-volume treasure altogether about eight inches thick. Yesterday, Charles G. Ross, the President's Secretary, was telling correspondents in confidence about the President's selection of the two Biblical texts. A Chicago newspaperman remarked that they made a mighty good program for a President. Today another reporter told the President about this. 'It is a good program,' replied Mr. Truman with emphasis. 'Especially the 10th Commandment. If you read the 10th it will do you a lot of good, especially in Washington.' In the White House texts issued today, the 10th Commandment was rendered as follows:

Thou shalt not covet thy neighbor's house, thou shalt not covet thy neighbor's wife, nor his manservant, nor his ox, nor his ass, nor anything that is thy neighbor's.

Dwight D. Eisenhower was sworn into office on January 21, 1953, on two inaugural Bibles, his own West Point (American Standard Version Bible) and Washington's Inaugural Bible. Eisenhower's Bible contains the following lines:

Presented to Dwight David Eisenhower upon his graduation from USMA, June, 1915.

II Chronicles 7:14, Eisenhower's choice of inaugural Scripture for his swearing in, is marked with a blue pencil:

If my people, who are called by my name, shall humble themselves and pray and seek my face, and turn from their wicked ways; then will I hear from heaven, and will forgive their sin, and will heal their land. (II Chronicles 7:14) American Standard Version

George Washington's inaugural Bible was simultaneously opened to Psalm 127 on this occasion:

Except the Lord build the house, they labor in vain that build it; except the Lord keep the city, the watchman waketh but in vain. It is vain for you to rise up early, to sit up late, to eat the bread of sorrows: for so he giveth his beloved sleep. Psalm 127:1-2

Eisenhower's second inauguration took place on January 21, 1957. At this time, the President's West Point Bible lay under his hand, his choice being the twelfth verse of the thirty-third Psalm:

Blessed is the nation whose God is Jehovah, The people whom he hath chosen for his own inheritance. Psalm 33:12

Richard Milhous Nixon was sworn into office on January 20, 1969. A *Washington Post* article of the same date gives us these details:

Mrs. Nixon will hold two family Bibles opened to Isaiah 2, verse 4, for her husband's oath-taking. The verse expresses the new President's hope that 'nation will beat their swords into plowshares, and their spears into pruning hooks' that 'nation shall not lift up sword against nation, neither shall they learn war anymore.'

January 20, 1973, marked Richard Nixon's second inauguration as first officer of the Executive Branch of our government. A *Washington Evening Star* article, dated January 21, 1973, covered the event as follows:

As he did four years ago, President Nixon spoke the oath with his left hand resting on two Nixon family Bibles, 100 and 145 years old. His wife Pat held them. Each was open to Isaiah 2:4, which speaks of nations that 'shall beat their swords into plowshares and their spears into pruning hooks, neither shall they learn war anymore.'

Gerald R. Ford was inaugurated as 38th President of the United States on August 9, 1974. Raising his right hand, Mr. Ford rested his left hand on a Bible held by his wife and opened to one of his favorite passages, the 5th and 6th verses of the 3rd Chapter of Proverbs:

> Trust in the Lord with all thine heart; and lean not unto thine own understanding. In all thy ways acknowledge Him and He shall direct thy paths.

Then, in a firm voice, he took the oath of office:

> I, Gerald Ford, do solemnly swear that I will faithfully execute the office of President of the United States and will to the best of my ability preserve, protect and defend the Constitution of the United States.

At his inaugural oath-taking ceremony, which took place on January 20, 1977, **James Earl Carter** made this observation:

> Here before me is the Bible used in the inauguration of our first President in 1789, and I have just taken the Oath of Office on the Bible my mother gave me just a few years ago, opened to a timeless admonition from the ancient prophet Micah: 'He hath showed thee O man, what is good, and what doth the Lord require of thee, but to do justly, and to love mercy, and to walk humbly with thy God.' Micah 6:8 (Excerpted from a *Washington Post* article dated January 21, 1977.)

On January 20, 1981 and January 20, 1985 respectively, **Ronald Reagan**, our 40th president, made his pledge of allegiance to the Constitution of the United States with his left hand upon his mother's Bible, the New Indexed Bible, King James Version, published by the Dickson Publishing Company in Chicago, Illinois; having selected her favorite Scripture verse:

> If my people, which are called by My name, shall humble themselves, and pray, and seek my face, and turn from their wicked ways; then will I hear from heaven, and will forgive their sin, and will heal their land. II Chronicles 7:14

I believe that the God of our founding fathers was speaking through the Presidential Inaugural Scripture chosen by Ronald Reagan, our fortieth First Officer, when he swore allegiance to the Constitution with the left hand upon the Bible, at his first and second inaugurations.

His mother wrote a sonnet inside the front cover of the Bible. It reads as follows:

When I consider how my life is spent
The most that I can do will be to prove
'Tis by His side, each day, I seek to move.
To higher, nobler things my mind is bent
Thus giving of my strength, which God has lent,
I strive some needy soul's unrest, to soothe
Lest they the paths of righteousness shall lose.
Through fault of mine, my Maker to present
If I should fail to show them of their needs
How would I hope to meet Him face to face,
Or give a just account of all my ways
In thought of mind, in word, and in each deed
My life must prove the power of His grace
By every action through my living days.

—Nellie Reagan

Within the Bible Mrs. Reagan wrote these notations:

If in sorrow, read John 14
If people fail you, read Ps. 27
If you worry, read Matt. 6:19, 37
If down-cast, read Ps. 34
If discouraged, read Isaiah 40
If your faith becomes weak, read Heb. 11

A Thought For Today:

You can be too big for God to use but you cannot be too small.

LESSON TWO

PUPILS' GUIDE

The U.S. Capitol - Legislative Branch of our Government

I. Suggestions for Study

    a)   Read the Lesson material carefully.

    b)   Look up La Rabida, Spain; Philadelphia, Pennsylvania; and Yorktown, Virginia on your map of the world at home.

II. Lesson Material

    Text: Lesson 2 - The U.S. Capitol - Legislative Branch of our Government.

III. 1. The kind of Nation that America is:

    i)   *The Genius of America* has her hope squarely based upon: (Circle one)

        a)   television

        b)   newspapers

        c)   justice

        d)   sports

    ii)   In *The Genius of America* sculpture: (Consult your text and fill in the blanks)

        a)   _____ America stands in the _____ with a _____ behind her, and a _____ bearing _____ upon it. Beneath the shield is inscribed _____ _____ _____. America gazes at _____ to the _____ who beckons her to _____ . However, America points towards _____ to the left, who holds a pair of _____ in her left _____ and a _____ in her right, reading: _____.

    iii)   Explain the message which the artist conveys in his masterpiece sculpture, *The Genius of America*. (Consult your text)

        a)   _____

            _____

            _____

            _____

iv) In the *Christopher Columbus Bronze Doorway*, the second landmark from the bottom, on the left-hand-side, depicts Christopher Columbus leaving: (Circle one)

    a)   A marketplace
    b)   A splendid mansion
    c)   A palace
    d)   A convent

v) Constantino Brumidi, political refugee from Rome, spent 25 years of his life painting scenes of America's history, flora and fauna in our U.S. Capitol. His purpose was: (Fill in the blanks)

    a)   "To make _____ the _____ of the one _____ on earth in which there is _____." This he did with _____ _____ to a _____ he _____; a _____ which had opened its arms_____to him in his_____ ____ _____.

vi) In the painting *The Signing of the Declaration of Independence, July 4th, 1776* by John Trumbull, the Declaration of Independence is presented by its author. His name is: (Fill in the blank)

    a)   _____.

The four founding fathers standing behind the author are: (Circle correct answers)

    a)   Patrick Henry
    b)   Roger Sherman
    c)   Robert Livingston
    d)   John Jay
    e)   John Adams
    f)   George Mason
    g)   Benjamin Franklin

vii) In Great Master artist John Trumbull's eye-witness painting, *Surrender of Lord Cornwallis at Yorktown, Virginia, October 19th, 1781*, the British, who are centrally represented, surrendered to: (Circle one)

    a)   Czar Nicolas I
    b)   Louis XIV of France
    c)   Charles II of England
    d)   George Washington, of the United States of America

viii) Great Master artist Howard Chandler Christy's painting, *Scene at the Signing of the Constitution of the United States* depicts how many signers of this foundational American document? (Circle one)

   a) 56
   b) 29
   c) 39
   d) 40

ix) In Great Master artist Howard Chandler Christy's painting, Robert Morris, portrayed to the right with his elbow upon the table, was: (Consult your text and fill in the blanks)

   a) The _____ of the _____ Revolution. The artist has depicted a _____ next to his elbow, opened at _____ _____ Chapter ____.

x) The above represents the fact that, in formulating the U.S. Constitution, America's founding fathers turned to: (Fill in the blanks)

   a) The Magna Carta
   b) Thomas Jefferson's Law books
   c) The Bible
   d) John Locke's Treaties

xi) There are 23 bas-relief sculptured faces of ancient law-makers of the past upon the inner walls of the U.S. House of Representatives. The sculpture directly facing the Speaker of the House's chair, in this chamber where binding laws are made, is that of: (Circle one)

   a) Blackstone of England
   b) King Louis IX of France
   c) Hammurabi
   d) Moses (Exodus 20)

xii) From whom, and where, did Moses obtain the law - The Ten Commandments? (Circle one)

   a) The government
   b) Israel's ruler
   c) Pharaoh of Egypt
   d) Almighty God, on Mount Sinai

xiii) The Congressional Prayer Room in the U.S. Capitol has a beautiful stained-glass window - *George Washington kneeling in Prayer at Valley Forge*. The Scripture verse inscribed around our first U.S. president, lost in prayer, is: (Circle one)

    a) Psalm 19:1
    b) Revelation 3:10
    c) Psalm 16:1
    d) Psalm 24:1

xiv) Underneath the figure of *George Washington Kneeling in Prayer at Valley Forge* are inscribed the words: (Circle one)

    a) Prosperity, peace and happiness
    b) This Nation, Under God
    c) United Nations
    d) Self-achievement

xv) What does this signify, in the Great Master artist's masterpiece of America's history? (Fill in the blanks)

    a) Beneath the figure _____ ____ _____, the _____ of the_____ _____ stands out, on the one hand depicting _____ and _____, and on the other, _____ to its _____ and _____ .

2. Christian Character Traits:

Select 10 Christian virtues, values and morals inherent within the sculpural, artistic and architectural themes of the U.S. Capitol. List them below:

a. _____   f. _____

b. _____   g. _____

c. _____   h. _____

d. _____   i. _____

e. _____   j. _____

IV. Illustrate your work with pictures, outline map, models and drawings.

V. Memory verse:

Preserve me, O God, for in Thee do I put my Trust. Psalm 16:1

The Supreme Court of the United States

The marble statue, "The Contemplation of Justice" by James Earle Fraser.

The Christian Heritage Of Our Nation - History Curriculum

Main, oak doorway to the Inner Courtroom – United States Supreme Court.
The Ten Commandments (Exodus 20), the only symbol upon these doors.

Marble bas-relief sculptured panel on the wall above the Bench, Inner Courtroom, Supreme Court of the United States. The Ten Commandments (Exodus 20), stand out in predominance above the Chief Justice's head – "The Power of Government" to the left, and "The Majesty of the Law" to the right.

The Christian Heritage Of Our Nation - History Curriculum

SECURITY   HARMONY   PEACE   CHARITY   DEFENSE of VIRTUE   WISDOM

"The Struggle between Good (depicted above) and Evil, with Good prevailing." Marble bas-relief sculptured panel, on the wall facing the Bench, Inner Courtroom, Supreme Court of the United States. Sculptor: Adolph Weinman.

"EVIL"

LIES AND DECEIT

SLANDER AND FALSE WITNESS

HYPOCRISY AND CORRUPTION

DESPOTIC POWER

"The Struggle between Good, and Evil (depicted above) with Good prevailing." Marble bas-relief sculptured panel, on the wall facing the Bench, Inner Courtroom, U.S. Supreme Court.

LIES AND DECEIT

After "The Triumph of Justice" bas-relief sculpture "The Struggle Between Good and Evil, with Good prevailing," by Adolf Weinman. Inner Chamber, U.S. Supreme Court.

The Christian Heritage Of Our Nation - History Curriculum

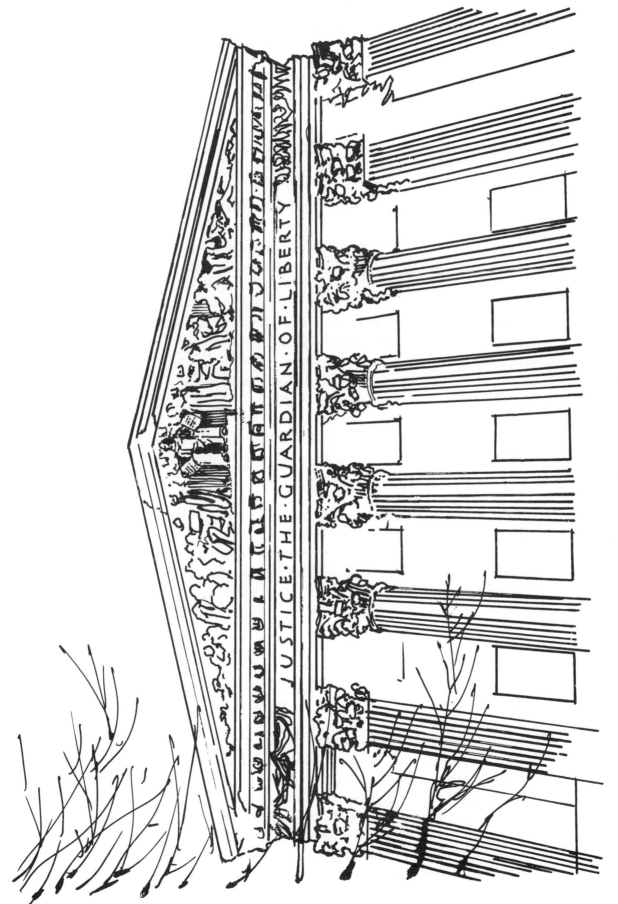

"Justice the Guardian of Liberty." East exterior facade, U.S. Supreme Court. Moses is the central, focal point, with two tablets of the Ten Commandments (Exodus 20), one in either hand.

LESSON 3

UNITED STATES SUPREME COURT -
JUDICIAL BRANCH OF OUR GOVERNMENT

Across from the Capitol grounds stands the Supreme Court of the United States. In 1791 the Supreme Court of the United States had its beginnings in a handsome red brick building of Georgian design, to the left of Independence Hall in Philadelphia. The first three Chief Justices – John Jay, John Rutledge and Oliver Ellesworth presided over this court, passing down decisions from its attractive courtroom. John Jay, first U.S. Supreme Court Chief Justice, was also the president of the American Bible Society. Jay had one hour of Bible reading with his family and servants each morning and evening.

In 1801, the Supreme Court moved to Washington, D.C., where it joined the newly-established government, being housed in various locations within the Capitol building until the grand opening of its present building in 1935. The exterior facade of the new building consists of white marble from Vermont. It was designed by Cass Gilbert to resemble a neoclassical Roman Temple. A seated figure entitled: *The Authority of Law*, to the right, and its female counterpart, *The Contemplation of Justice*, to the left, flank the main steps to its entrance. James Earle Fraser was the sculptor of these two statues. The female statue is carved from a single piece of marble weighing fifty tons.

A letter addressed to the Architect of the Capitol dated February 12, 1942, gives Fraser's description of his creation as follows:

> The figure is enveloped in thought. The small statue she holds at her side is the symbol of justice which indicates on what she is thinking. . . it is a realistic conception of what I consider a heroic type of person with a head and body expressive of the beauty and intelligence of justice.[26]

One gains access to the inner courtroom through a majestic oak doorway. Each door has beautifully engraved upon its lower half the Ten Commandments of Almighty God. (Exodus 20)

The Inner Courtroom of the Supreme Court shows four marble bas-relief panels beneath the ceiling on each of the four walls. Each has a particular story to tell. The panel directly above the bench where Chief Justice William Rhenquist and the eight Associate Justices are seated, depicts *The Power of Government,* and *The Majesty of the Law*. Between these two allegorical figures, the Ten Commandments stand out in a position of prominence. The seated figure representing *The Power of Government* has his elbow squarely resting upon God's Ten Commandments, showing from whence our power is derived. Directly facing the scene, on the opposite wall, a struggle between good and evil is depicted, with Security, Harmony, Peace, Charity, and Defense of

Virtue triumphing over Corruption, Slander, Deceit and Despotic Power. This marble bas-relief panel is entitled: *The Struggle Between Good and Evil, with Good Prevailing.* The sculptor has personified God's good versus Satan's evil with his characters, who could well be taken out of Galatians 5:22-23. It depicts a clash between God's virtues and laws, or the fruit of the Holy Spirit, and the evil works of Satan. Both marble sculptures in the Inner Courtroom of the Supreme Court, highest court in the land, stand out as awesome reminders that truly we are a Christian nation.

East Facade of Supreme Court

Justice, the Guardian of Liberty, is the title to the East pediment of the building. A stark reminder of the origin and basis for our American legal system is depicted in the central figure of Moses holding the two tablets of the Old Testament Law, one in either hand.

The Book of the Law, or the Pentateuch, as it is also called, comprises the first five books of the Old Testament: Genesis, Exodus, Leviticus, Numbers and Deuteronomy. God promised unfailing loyalty and love to Joshua, just as He had shown to His servant Moses.

A recurring theme of the Old Testament is success and prosperity based upon meditation and constant striving to abide by the perfect Law of God. The New Testament, being a fulfillment of the Old, only reinforces God's words. The Messiah Himself states that He did not come to abolish the Law but to fulfill it: ". . . not the smallest jot or tittle shall pass away from the Law, until all is accomplished." (Matthew 5:17,18) The jot and tittle are the tiniest markings in the Hebrew alphabet.

The United States a Christian Nation

Supreme Court Justice David J. Brewer, who served from 1890-1910, gave a magnificent lecture entitled *The United States a Christian Nation,* which is hereunder excerpted. This brilliant American statesman dealt with the subject from every conceivable aspect—academic, educational, legal, constitutional, cultural, economic, executive, biblical and symbolic—leaving no stone unturned:

> We classify nations in various ways, as, for instance, by their form of government. One is a kingdom, another an empire, and still another a republic. Also by race. Great Britain is an Anglo-Saxon nation, France a Gallic, Germany a Teutonic, Russia a Slav. And still again others are heathen, and still others are Christian nations.
>
> This Republic is classified among the Christian nations of the world. It was so formally declared by the Supreme Court of the United States. In the case of Holy Trinity Church vs. United States, 143 U.S. 471, that Court, after mentioning various circumstances, added, "these and many other matters which might be noticed, add a volume of unofficial declarations to the mass of

organic utterances that this is a Christian nation." (Unanimous opinion, Feb. 29, 1892) But in what sense can it be called a Christian nation? Not in the sense that Christianity is the established religion or that the people are in any manner compelled to support it. On the contrary, the Constitution specifically provides that "Congress shall make no law respecting an establishment of religion, or prohibiting the free exercise thereof." Neither is it Christian in the sense that all its citizens are either in fact or name Christians. On the contrary, all religions have free scope within our borders. Numbers of our people profess other religions, and many reject all. Nor is it Christian in the sense that a profession of Christianity is condition to holding office or otherwise engaging in the public service, or essential to recognition either politically or socially. In fact the Government as a legal organization is independent of all religions.

Nevertheless, we constantly speak of this Republic as a Christian nation—in fact, as the leading Christian nation of the world. This popular use of the term certainly has significance. It is not a mere creation of the imagination. It is not a term of derision but has substantial basis—one which justifies its use. Let us analyze a little and see what is the basis.

Its use has had from the early settlements on our shores and still has an official foundation. It is only about three centuries since the beginning of civilized life within the limits of these United States. And those beginnings were in a marked and marvelous degree identified with Christianity. . .

Christianity Inspired Colonies

It is not an exaggeration to say that Christianity in some of its creeds was the principal cause of the settlement of many of the colonies, and co-operated with business hopes and purposes in the settlement of the others. Beginning in this way and under these influences it is not strange that the colonial life had an emphatic Christian tone. . .

In Delaware, by the Constitution of 1776, every officeholder was required to make and subscribe the following declaration: "I, A.B., do profess faith in God the Father, and in Jesus Christ His Only Son, and in the Holy Ghost, one God, blessed forevermore; and I do acknowledge the Holy Scriptures of the Old and New Testament to be given by divine inspiration."

New Hampshire, in the Constitutions of 1784 and 1792, required that senators and representatives should be of the "Protestant religion." And this provision remained in force until 1877.

The fundamental Constitutions of the Carolinas declared: "No man shall be permitted to be a freeman of Carolina, or to have any estate or habitation within it that doth not acknowledge a God, and that God is publicly and solemnly to be worshipped."

The Constitution of North Carolina, of 1776 provided: "That no person who shall deny the being of God or the truth of the Protestant religion, or the

The Christian Heritage Of Our Nation - History Curriculum

divine authority either of the Old or New Testaments, or who shall hold religious principles incompatible with the freedom and safety of the State, shall be capable of holding any office or place of trust or profit in the civil department within this State." And this remained in force until 1835, when it was amended by changing the word "Protestant" to "Christian," and as so amended remained in force until the Constitution of 1868. And in that Constitution among the persons disqualified for office were "all persons who shall deny the being of Almighty God.". . .

Christianity Fundamental to Office Holding

In Maryland, by the Constitution of 1776, every person appointed to any office of profit or trust was not only to take an official oath of allegiance to the State, but also to "subscribe a declaration of his belief in the Christian religion." In the same State, in the Constitution of 1851, it was declared that no other test or qualification for admission to any office of trust or profit shall be required than the official oath "and a declaration of belief in the Christian religion; and if the party shall profess to be a Jew the declaration shall be of his belief in a future state of rewards and punishments." As late as 1864 the same State in its Constitution had a similar provision, the change being one merely of phraseology, the provision reading, "a declaration of belief in the Christian religion, or of the existence of God, and in a future state of rewards and punishments."

Mississippi by the Constitution of 1817, provided that "no person who denies the being of God or a future state of rewards and punishments shall hold any office in the civil department of the State."

Another significant matter is the recognition of Sunday. That day is the Christian Sabbath, a day peculiar to that faith, and known to no other. It would be impossible within the limits of a lecture to point out all the ways in which that day is recognized. The following illustrations must suffice: By the United States Constitution the President is required to approve all bills passed by Congress. If he disapproves he returns it with his veto. And then specifically it is provided that if not returned by him within ten days, "Sundays excepted, . . ." after it shall have been presented to him it becomes a law. Similar provisions are found in the Constitutions of most of the States, and in thirty-six out of forty-five is the same expression, "Sundays excepted. . ."

By decisions in many states a contract made on Sunday is invalid and cannot be enforced. By the general course of decision no judicial proceedings can be held on Sunday. All legislative bodies, whether municipal, state or national, abstain from work on that day. Indeed, the vast number of official actions, legislative and judicial, recognizes Sunday as a day separate and apart from the others, a day devoted not to the ordinary pursuits of life. . . .

God's Name Prevails

While the word "God" is not infrequently used both in the singular and plural to denote any supreme being or beings, yet when used alone and in the singular number it generally refers to that Supreme Being spoken of in the Old and New Testaments and worshipped by Jew and Christian. In that sense the word is used in constitution, statute and instrument. In many State Constitutions we find in the preamble a declaration like this: "Grateful to Almighty God." In some he who denied the being of God was disqualified from holding office. It is again and again declared in constitution and statute that official oaths shall close with an appeal, "So help me, God." When, upon inauguration, the President-elect each four years consecrates himself to the great responsibilities of Chief Executive of the Republic, his vow of consecration in the presence of the vast throng filling the Capitol grounds will end with the solemn words, "So help me, God." In all our courts witnesses in like manner vouch for the truthfulness of their testimony. The common commencement of wills is "In the name of God, Amen." Every foreigner attests his renunciation of allegiance to his former sovereign and his acceptance of citizenship in this Republic by an appeal to God.

These various declarations in charters, constitutions and statutes indicate the general thought and purpose. If it be said that similar declarations are not found in all the charters or in all the constitutions, it will be borne in mind that the omission oftentimes was because they were deemed unnecessary, as shown by the quotation just made from the opinion of the Supreme Court of Louisiana, as well as those hereafter taken from the opinions of other courts. And further, it is of still more significance that there are no contrary declarations. In no charter or constitution is there anything to even suggest that any other than the Christian is the religion of this country. In none of them is Mohammed or Confucius or Buddha in any manner noticed. In none of them is Judaism recognized other than by way of toleration of its special creed. While the separation of church and state is often affirmed, there is nowhere a repudiation of Christianity as one of the institutions as well as benedictions of society.

In short, there is no charter or constitution that is either infidel, agnostic or anti-Christian. Wherever there is a declaration in favor of any religion it is of the Christian. In view of the multitude of expressions in its favor, the avowed separation between church and state is a most satisfactory testimonial that it is the religion of this country, for a peculiar thought of Christianity is of a personal relation between man and his Maker, uncontrolled by and independent of human government.

Notice also the matter of chaplains. These are appointed for the army and navy, named as officials of legislative assemblies, and universally they belong to one or other of the Christian denominations. Their whole range of service, whether in prayer or preaching, is an official recognition of Christianity. If it be not so, why do we have chaplains?

Christ Honored in All States

If we consult the decisions of the courts, although the formal question has seldom been presented because of a general recognition of its truth, yet in The People vs Ruggles, 8 John. 290,294,295, Chancellor Kent, the great commentator on American law, speaking as Chief Justice of the Supreme Court of New York, said: "The people of this State, in common with the people of this country, profess the general doctrines of Christianity, as the rule of their faith and practice. . ."

The New York Supreme Court, in Lindenmuller vs. The People, 33 Barbour, 561, held that: "Christianity is not the legal religion of the State, as established by law. If it were, it would be a civil or political institution, which it is not; but this is not inconsistent with the ideal that it is in fact, and ever has been, the religion of the people. This fact is everywhere prominent in all our civil and political history, and has been, from the first, recognized and acted upon by the people, as well as by constitutional conventions, by legislatures and by courts of justice. . ."

In Arkansas, Shover vs. The State, 10 English, 263, the Supreme Court said: "This system of religion (Christianity) is recognized as constituting a part and parcel of the common law. . ."

If now we pass from the domain of official action and recognition to that of individual acceptance we enter a field of boundless extent, and I can only point out a few of the prominent facts: Notice our educational institutions. I have already called your attention to the provisions of the charters of the first three colleges. Think of the vast number of academies, colleges and universities scattered through the land. Some of them it is true, are under secular control, but there is yet to be established in this country one of those institutions founded on the religions of Confucius, Buddha or Mohammed, while an overwhelming majority are under the special direction and control of Christian teachers. . .

The Bible, the Guide to Life

You will have noticed that I have presented no doubtful facts. Nothing has been stated which is debatable. The quotations from charters are in the archives of the several States; the laws are on the statute books; judicial opinions are taken from the official reports; statistics from the census publications. In short, no evidence has been presented which is open to question. I could easily enter upon another line of examination. I could point out of the general trend of public opinion, the disclosures of purposes and beliefs to be found in letters, papers, books and unofficial declarations. I could show how largely our laws and customs are based upon the laws of Moses and the teachings of Christ; how constantly the Bible is appealed to as the guide to life and the authority in questions of morals; how the Christian doctrines are accepted as the great comfort in times of sorrow and affliction, and fill with the light of hope the services for the dead. On every hilltop towers the steeple of some Christian church while from the marble witnesses in God's acre comes the universal but silent testimony to the common faith in the Christian doctrine of the resurrection and the life hereafter.

But I must not weary you. I could go on indefinitely, pointing out further illustrations both official and non-official, public and private; such as the annual Thanksgiving proclamations, with their following days of worship and feasting; announcements of days of fasting and prayer; the universal celebration of Christmas; the gathering of millions of our children in Sunday Schools, and the countless volumes of Christian literature, both prose and poetry. But I have said enough to show that Christianity came to this country with the first colonists; has been powerfully identified with its rapid development, colonial and national, and today exists as a mighty factor in the life of the Republic. This is a Christian nation. . .

It behooves us to complete this chapter on the Supreme Court with a poignant message inscribed above the main, Pennsylvania Avenue Entrance to the *Department of Justice* building. It encapsulates the application of The Ten Commandments to each and every life:

Justice in the Life and Conduct of the State is possible only
as first it Resides in the Hearts and Souls of the Citizens.

LESSON THREE

PUPILS' GUIDE

The U.S. Supreme Court –
Judicial Branch of Our Government

I. Suggestions for Study

a) Read the Lesson material carefully.
b) Look up Philadelphia, PA. and Washington, D.C. on your map of the U.S. at home.

II. Lesson Material

Text: Lesson 3 - The Supreme Court of the United States.

III. 1. The kind of Nation that America is:

i) The two famous statues on either side of the front entranceway to the U.S. Supreme Court are entitled: (Fill in the blanks)

a) _____ and   b) _____

ii) In sculptor James Earle Fraser's February 12, 1942 letter to the Architect of the Capitol, he states of *The Contemplation of Justice*: (Consult your text and fill in the blanks)

a) The figure is enveloped in _____ . The small statue she holds at her side is the symbol of _____, which indicates on what she is thinking. . .It is a _____ conception of what I consider a _____ type of _____ with a _____ and _____ expressive of the _____ and _____ of justice.

iii) What is the only symbol upon each inner door, of the main oak doorway leading into the Inner Courtroom of the U.S. Supreme Court?

a) The Code of Hammurabi
b) Jupiter
c) The Ten Commandments (Exodus 20)
d) A greek goddess

iv) What is the central, predominant symbol sculptured directly above the Chief Justice's head, in the Inner Courtroom of the U.S. Supreme Court? (Circle one)

    a) The Koran
    b) A Menorah
    c) Zeus
    d) The Ten Commandments (Exodus 20)

v) The two sculptured figures on either side of the central, predominant symbol above the Chief Justice's head - Inner Courtroom of the U.S. Supreme Court, are entitled: (Fill in the blanks)

    a) _____ and _____

    b) *The Power of Government* has his left elbow squarely and confidently resting upon the stability and security of: (Circle one)

        i) U.S. Congressmen
        ii) The President
        iii) The Ten Commandments of Almighty God (Exodus 20)
        iv) Nine U.S. Supreme Court Justices

vi) In Great Master sculptor Adolph Weinman's masterpiece, opposite the Bench: *The Struggle Between Good and Evil with Good Prevailing*, the characters representing *Good* are: (Circle all correct answers)

    a) Security
    b) Error
    c) Cheating
    d) Harmony
    e) Disobedience
    f) Peace
    g) Chaos
    h) Rebellion
    i) Ingratitude
    j) Charity
    k) Anarchy
    l) Defense of Virtue
    m) Selfishness
    n) Wisdom

vii)   In Great Master sculptor Adolph Weinman's masterpiece, *The Struggle between Good and Evil with Good Prevailing* opposite the Bench, the characters representing *Evil* are: (Circle all correct answers)

   a)   Discernment
   b)   Reproof
   c)   Correction
   d)   Lies and Deceit
   e)   Discipline
   f)   Admonition
   g)   Slander and False witness
   h)   Chastisement
   i)   Hypocrisy
   j)   Meekness
   k)   Despotic power
   l)   Corruption

viii) In Adolf Weinman's masterpiece, the central, focal sculpture between *Good* to the left and *Evil* to the right is entitled: (Circle one)

   a)   Evil reigns
   b)   Protect the environment
   c)   The Triumph of Justice
   d)   Peace, Happiness and Prosperity

ix)   Sculptor Herman McNeil's marble sculptured masterpiece on the outer, east facade of the U.S. Supreme Court is entitled: (Circle one)

   a)   Federal Government Building
   b)   Liberty reigns Supreme
   c)   Justice the Guardian of Liberty
   d)   We, the People

x)   The central figure in the sculptured pediment on the outer, east facade of the U.S. Supreme Court, directly above the Chief Justice's head on the outside is: (Circle one)

   a)   Hammurabi
   b)   Confucius
   c)   Solon
   d)   Moses and the Ten Commandments (Exodus 20)

xi)   Explain the significance of the predominant symbol on the east facade of the U.S. Supreme Court, directly above the Chief Justice's head on the outside. (Consult your text and fill in the blanks)

a) A stark _____ of the _____ and _____ for our_____ _____ _____ is depicted in the _____ figure of _____ holding the two _____ of the _____ _____ _____, one in either hand.

2. *Christian Character Traits:*

Select 10 Christian virtues, values and morals woven into the art, sculpture and inscriptions pertaining to the United States Supreme Court. List them below:

a. _____   f. _____

b. _____   g. _____

c. _____   h. _____

d. _____   i. _____

e. _____   j. _____

IV. Illustrate your work with pictures, outline map, models and drawings.

V. Memory verses: Exodus 20:1-18

The Ten Commandments

I.	Thou shalt have none other gods but Me.
II.	Thou shalt not make to thyself any graven image.
III.	Thou shalt not take the name of the Lord thy God in vain.
IV.	Remember that thou keep holy the Sabbath day.
V.	Honour thy father and thy mother.
VI.	Thou shalt do no murder.
VII.	Thou shalt not steal.
VIII.	Thou shalt not commit adultery.
IX.	Thou shalt not bear false witness against thy neighbour.
X.	Thou shalt not covet.

(As inscribed above the altar in the 1607 Jamestown settlers' church, Jamestown Island, Virginia).

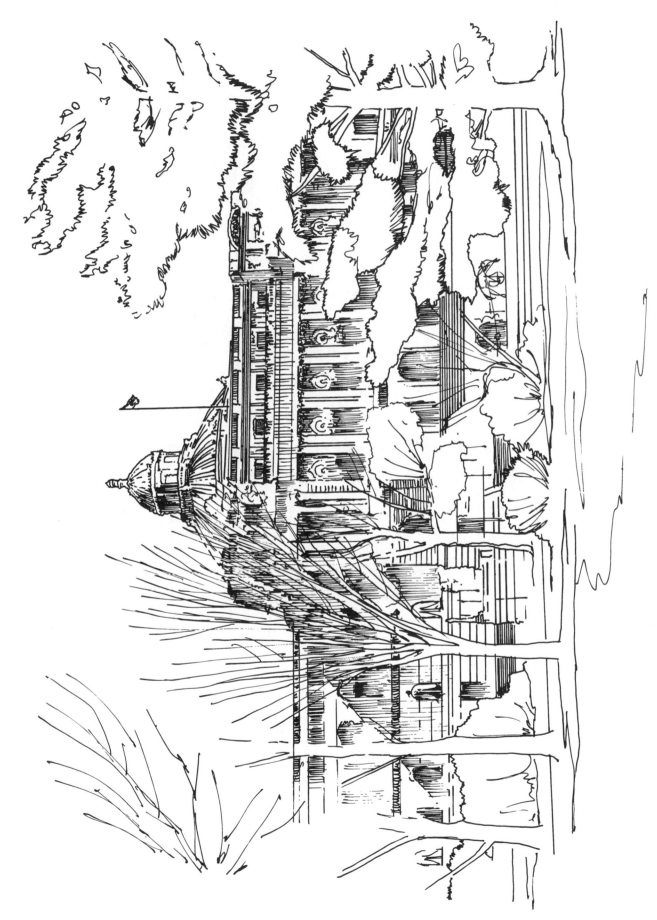

Library of Congress – Historic Thomas Jefferson Building, 1897

The "Torch of Learning" atop the dome, Library of Congress Main Reading Room, historic Thomas Jefferson building.

The Christian Heritage Of Our Nation - History Curriculum

*The sculptured face of Benjamin Franklin stands out above the
Main Entranceway to the Library of Congress, Thomas Jefferson building.*

The Main Vestibule, Library of Congress Thomas Jefferson building, called "The Most Beautiful Building in the World" at its opening in 1897.

The Christian Heritage Of Our Nation - History Curriculum

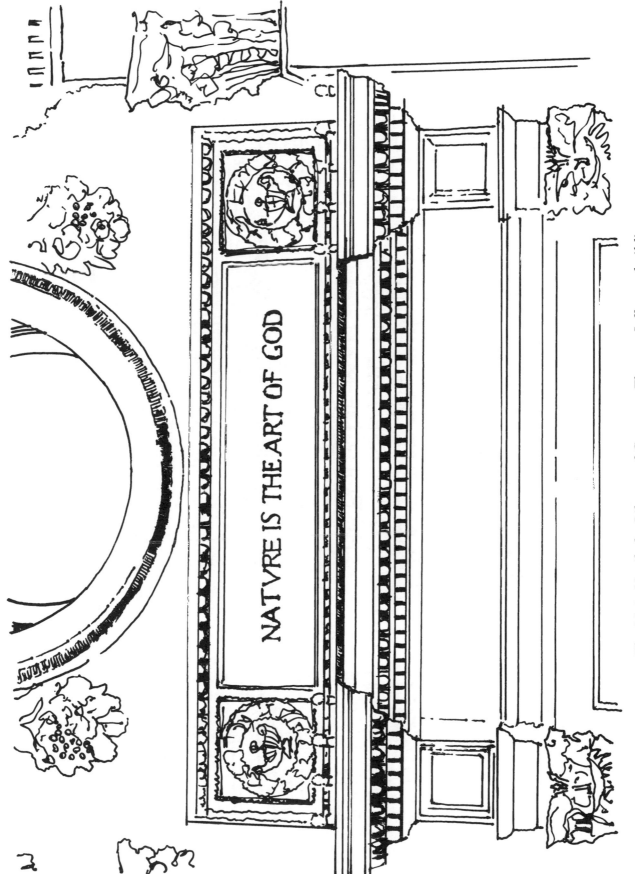

NATVRE IS THE ART OF GOD

The Main Vestibule, Library of Congress Thomas Jefferson building.

The Main Vestibule, Library of Congress Thomas Jefferson building. The above inscription can be equated with the Apostle Paul's words to the Corinthians that "The body is a Temple of the Holy Spirit." I Corinthians 6:19.

THERE IS BVT ONE TEMPLE
IN THE VNIVERSE AND THAT IS
THE BODY OF MAN

The Christian Heritage Of Our Nation - History Curriculum

HOW CHARMING IS DIVINE PHILOSOPHY.

The Main Vestibule, Library of Congress Thomas Jefferson building.

The Gutenberg Bible, 1455 A.D. On permanent exhibition at the Library of Congress.

The Christian Heritage Of Our Nation - History Curriculum

The Giant Bible of Mainz, 1453 A.D. On permanent exhibition at the Library of Congress.

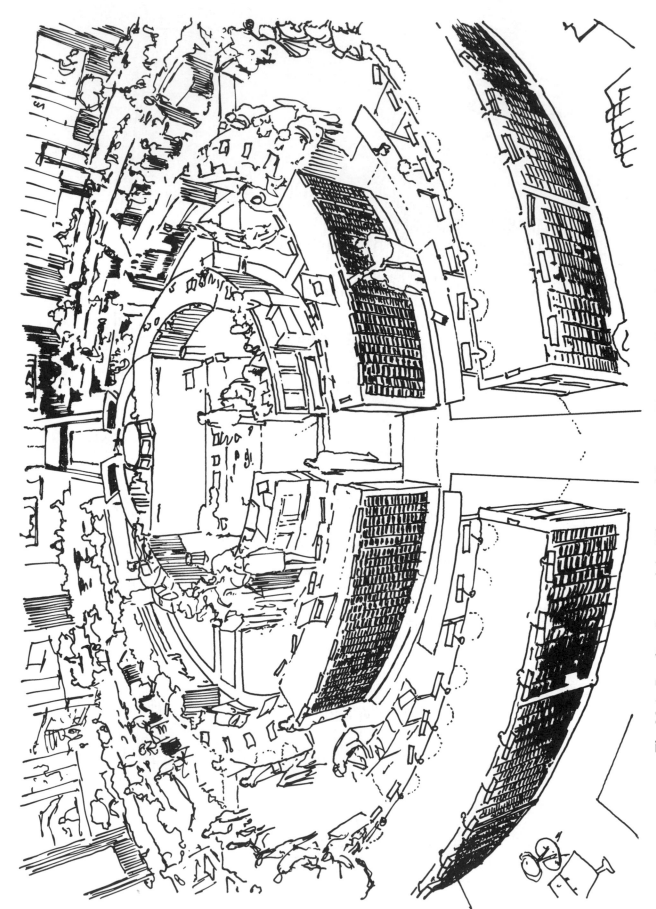

The Main Reading Room of the Library of Congress Thomas Jefferson building houses the Main Card Catalog, the Library's major scholarship tool, comprising more than 25 million cards.

The Christian Heritage Of Our Nation - History Curriculum

The statue "Religion." Main Reading Room,
Library of Congress Thomas Jefferson building. Micah 6:8.

Moses holding the two tablets of the Ten Commandments,
represents The Old Testament to the right of the statue "Religion."

The Christian Heritage Of Our Nation - History Curriculum

Paul, Apostle to the Gentiles, represents the New Testament (to the left of "Religion"). He holds "the Sword of the Spirit," the Word of God, in one hand, and the Scriptures in the other.

THE HEAVENS DECLARE
THE GLORY OF GOD.
AND THE FIRMAMENT
SHOWETH HIS HANDIWORK

The statue "Science," Main Reading Room, Library of Congress Thomas Jefferson building.

The Christian Heritage Of Our Nation - History Curriculum

"Judea - Religion" Inner Dome of the
Main Reading Room, Library of Congress Thomas Jefferson building.

LESSON 4

THE LIBRARY OF CONGRESS - LARGEST REPOSITORY OF AMERICANISM

Atop our national Library of Congress stands the *Torch of Learning,* welcoming all who wish to inquire into the vast array of knowledge which this library has to offer.

Benjamin Franklin founded the Library Company of Philadelphia in 1731 for the *Advancement of Knowledge and Literature.* It was a key intellectual resource for those who formed the Continental Congress, members of the Constitutional Convention and senators and representatives of the Congress of the United States. It served as America's first "Library of Congress" from 1774 until 1800, when Congress established our present-day Library of Congress, with an appropriation of five thousand dollars.

The library serves primarily as a research arm for Congress. Housed in a small chamber within the Capitol building, its collection at the outset comprised a mere 740 volumes and three maps.[27] During the 1812-1814 war, fire destroyed the young library's entire collection. With undaunted perseverance, the library purchased 6,700 books from the private collection of Thomas Jefferson, which this founding father sacrificially gave to Congress, at their own price, to compensate for the licentious barbarism of the British. On Christmas Eve, 1851, however, a second fire destroyed the larger part of this valuable new acquisition. Far from being deterred in its original plan and purpose, the Library of Congress commenced anew. Today, it estimates an approximate collection of 100 million items. Rare book collections (such as those belonging to founding father Thomas Jefferson; and Tsar Nicholas II); music, recordings, prints, photographs and copyright items are part of the collection.[28] The Rare Book Collection of the Libary of Congress is valued at four billion dollars.

Over 50 painters, sculptors, and artists were employed in the creation of the present building, which earned for itself the reputation of "the most beautiful building in the world," at its inauguration in 1897. Eight pillars adorn the inner sanctum of the Main Reading Room. Four of these extol God's greatness. Inscribed above the pillar representing Religion we read:

> What doth the Lord require of thee but to do justly, to love mercy and to walk humbly with thy God? (Micah 6:8)

Science bears these choice words:

> The heavens declare the glory of God and the firmament showeth His handiwork. (Psalm 19:1)

History formulates the following epitaph:

One God, one law, one element and one far-off Divine event to which the whole creation moves. (Alfred, Lord Tennyson)

Philosophy has coined its own descriptive words in the language of Bacon:

The inquiry, knowledge and belief of Truth is the sovereign good of human nature. (Francis Bacon)

Two magnificent bronze statues flank *Religion* on either side. They are *Moses* for the Old Testament, and *Paul, Apostle to the Gentiles* for the New.

The beautiful dome comprises hundreds of lotus flowers, gilded with 23-carat gold. A painting in the dome depicts past world civilizations and their major contribution to present-day world culture. Among these are: America, whose contribution is Science; Italy - Fine Arts; Germany - the Art of Printing; France - Emancipation; and Judea - Religion. Why religion? Because the Messiah, God's greatest gift to the world, came from Judea. An Israeli woman is portrayed next to this inscription with her hands raised in prayer and praise to Almighty God, the Ten Commandments by her side and the Old Testament Law on her lap.

Two of the world's oldest and most valuable Bibles are on display in the vestibule of this magnificent building. The Gutenberg Bible (1455 A.D.) was the first great Book printed with movable metal type. The library's copy is one of the three vellum copies in existence today. It was acquired through an Act of Congress as part of a private collection belonging to Mr. Otto Volbergh, living in Nazi Germany during the years preceding World War II. In fair exchange for this valuable heritage, his request for a passport to the United States and one and a half million dollars was granted. The Giant Bible of Mainz (1453 A.D.) holds its own unique position of preeminence as a hand-copied masterpiece of exceptional craftsmanship and ingenuity. Fifteen months of meticulous calligraphy demonstrates the scribe's painstaking effort in the completion of his God-given task.

Main Vestibule of the Library of Congress

Charles W. Eliot, former president of Harvard University was the sole consultant for the writings on the walls and ceilings. The Main Vestibule walls and ceilings radiate Christian, patriotic and traditional American themes in their inscriptions and paintings, such as the mural painting entitled "THE FAMILY. A mother holds, with outstretched arms, her babe who welcomes his father returning from the hunt. Grandparents and two older sisters beaming with affection complete the group." Other inscriptions glorify God, such as: "Nature is the Art of God" (Thomas Browne); "There is but one Temple in the Universe and that is the body of man" (Novalis); and "How charming is Divine Philosophy" (Milton). Another magnificent mural painting is entitled: "The Manuscript." It forms part of "The Evolution of the Book" wall paintings by John W. Alexander, and shows monastic scribes engrossing and illuminating biblical manuscripts in the Middle Ages. The last of these is "The Printing Press" of Johann Gutenberg, whose breakthrough in printing produced our famed *Gutenberg Bible*. The Main Vestibule portrays 26 beautifully sculptured cherubs lining both sides of the exquisite white marble stairwells which lead to the Mezzanine level and Visitors' Gallery. The work of sculptor Martiny, each cherub represents a different discipline, such as the cherub of "art," with a pallet; the cherub of "agriculture," with a sheaf of wheat; the cherub of "music," with a lyre and music book; the cherub of the vineyard with grapes, etc. Throughout the Main Reading Room and Main Vestibule are sculptured angels and cherubim, of which the Scriptures abound. They give God all the glory.

The Government of the Republic

The Lobby of the Main Reading Room main entranceway (in the Great Vestibule) shows forth five panels by Elihu Vedder. They symbolize "The Government of the Republic" and the results of good and bad administration. The panel of Government is above the beautiful main doors to the *Main Reading Room*. On the right are Good Administration, Peace and Prosperity; on the left, Corrupt Legislation and Anarchy. Government holds in her left hand a scepter and in her right hand a tablet upon which are inscribed Lincoln's words from his famed Gettysburg Address: "A Government of the people, by the people and for the people."

The Seals of the United States and Executive Departments

Altogether synonymous with the Americanism of this building, are patriotic themes, such as that of George W. Maynard's "The Discovery and Settlement of America." Portrayed in the ceiling are Courage, Valor, Fortitude and Achievement (Southwest Pavilion, Second Floor). And the seals of the United States and Executive Departments are large motifs on the walls and ceiling of the Second Floor North West Pavilion. The work of W.B. van Ingen and E.E. Garnsey, they are: "Treasury and State," with George Washington's inscribed words: " 'Tis our true policy to steer clear of permanent alliances with any portion of the foreign world," and Webster's "Let our object be our country, our whole country and nothing but our country." "Thank God! I also am an American."; "War and Navy," with inscriptions quoted from George Washington – "The aggregate happiness of society is, or ought to be, the end of all government." "To be prepared for war is one of the most effective means of preserving peace."; and "Justice and Post Office." In the central inner dome is the great seal of the United States. Forty-eight stars for America's 48 states, adorn the U.S. flag. Encircling the whole are Lincoln's famed words: "That this nation under God shall have a new birth of freedom."

The Representatives' Reading Room

To crown this building's reflection of godly Truth, are the ceiling paintings of the Representatives' Reading Room (South curtain). There are seven Lights of Civilization and their poignant meanings, as follows: *Indigo*—Light of Science; *Blue*—Light of

Truth (The Spirit of Truth is trampling the dragon of Error. The figures in the corners hold the Bible); *Green*—Light of Research; *Yellow*—Light of Creation (The Creator, Almighty God is depicted with His Word: "Let there be light" Genesis 1:1); *Orange*— Light of Progress; *Red*— Light of Poetry; *Violet*—Light of State is that of the Republic. America supports the shield of the United States, her liberty cap is inscribed 1776. She is attended by an eagle. In the border are mottoes, "Liberty, Suffrage, Justice and Fraternity."

Forty Great American Heroes

Woven into the mosaic ceiling above the *only two* permanent exhibits of the Main Vestibule—*The Gutenberg Bible* and *The Great Bible of Mainz* —are giants of America's Christian history, such as Jonathan Edwards and Cotton Mather; the nation's foremost sculptors and architects, such as Thomas Crawford (who sculpted "Armed Freedom" atop the U.S. Capitol dome); Thomas U. Walter (who designed the U.S. Capitol dome); and Benjamin LaTrobe, one of the U.S. Capitol's greatest architects, who also designed "the Church of the Presidents" in 1816. Also featured are Hiram Powers (who sculpted "Faith, Hope and Charity") and Gilbert Stuart, whose celebrated portrait of George Washington hangs in the East Room of the White House. Some of America's greatest composers, such as Louis Moreau Gottschalk (the first person to incorporate American musical themes into symphonic orchestration), also find their place among the 40 Americans representing our religious, artistic and scientific heritage.

Quotations from two great literary geniuses, namely, Henry David Thoreau's "Books are the Treasured Wealth of the World"; and Milton's "A Good Book is the Lifeblood of a Master Spirit," in gold lettering, stand out to either side of the inner, main bronze doorway of the Main Vestibule, the interior of which has been described as "a vision in polished stone."

LESSON FOUR

Library of Congress of the United States – Largest Repository of Americanism

I. Suggestions for Study

a) Read the Lesson material carefully.

b) Look up Washington, D.C.; Boston, Massachusetts; Mainz, Germany and Judea, Israel on your map of the world at home.

II. Lesson Material

Text: Lesson 4 - The Library of Congress of the United States.

III. I. The Kind of Nation America is:

i) Atop our national Library of Congress 1897 Thomas Jefferson building, stands: (Consult text and fill in the blanks)

    a) "The_____ of_____," welcoming_____who wish to_____into the vast_____of_____which this _____has to_____.

ii) This library serves primarily as: (Circle one)

    a) A repository for world literature and culture
    b) A research arm for U.S. Congress
    c) A government storage-house
    d) A museum

iii) How many painters, sculptors and artists were employed in the creation of the 1897 historic Thomas Jefferson building? (Circle one)

    a) 10
    b) 15
    c) 25
    d) 50

iv) Why is the sculptured face of founding father, Benjamin Franklin centrally featured above the Main Entranceway of the historic 1897 Library of Congress Thomas Jefferson building? Because Benjamin Franklin was: (Circle one)

    a) A philanthropist
    b) A scientist

      c)   Its founder

      d)   An inventor

v)   Who initially founded our national Library of Congress, and when? (Circle one)

      a)   Thomas Jefferson in 1776

      b)   Benjamin Franklin in 1731

      c)   George Washington in 1781

      d)   John Adams in 1799

vi)   What was the original name of the Library of Congress, and where was it founded? (Circle one)

      a)   The Congressional Bureaucracy, in Washington, D.C.

      b)   The Library Company, in Philadelphia

      c)   The President's Library, at Princeton

      d)   The Athenaeum, in Boston

vii)   Why did the founder of our national Library of Congress establish this library? (Circle one)

      a)   For entertainment and the media

      b)   For the encouragement of hobbies

      c)   For the Advancement of Knowledge and Literature

      d)   For craftsmanship and folklore

viii)   The Main Vestibule of the Library of Congress Thomas Jefferson building, reflects the reputation, at its inauguration in 1897, of: (Circle one)

      a)   A mausoleum

      b)   An art gallery

      c)   "The most Beautiful building in the World"

      d)   A spacious reception room for government bureaucrats

ix)   Five of the numerous inscriptions glorifying God upon the inner walls of the Library of Congress Main Vestibule, and the Main Reading Room, read: (Fill in the blanks)

      a)   Nature is the _____ of_____ . (Thomas Browne)

      b)   How_____is_____ philosophy. (Milton)

      c)   One____ , one_____,one_____,one far off_____event, to whom the whole_____ moves. (Alfred, Lord Tennyson)

d) What doth ____ _____ require of thee, but to do _____, to love_____, and to walk_____ with thy God. (Micah 6:8)

e) The _____ declare the _____ of _____ and the _____ showeth His_____. (Psalm 19:1)

x) What is the most valuable book in our national Library of Congress collection? (Circle one)

a) Adolph Hitler's Memoirs
b) Thomas Jefferson's original draft of the Declaration of Independence
c) The Gutenberg Bible, 1455 A.D.
d) Christopher Columbus' Book of Prophecies

xi) The Main Card Catalogue of the Library of Congress comprises: (Fill in the blanks)

a) More than _____ million _____ representing the largest _____ of true_____ in the world.

xii) The Rare Book Collection of the Library of Congress comprises two card catalogues, representing original, one-of-a-kind books on America's foundations as a nation under God. It is valued at: (Circle one)

a) One million dollars
b) Twenty million dollars
c) Four billion dollars
d) Seventy million dollars

xiii) The two bronze statues on either side of the statue *Religion* in the Main Reading Room of our national Library of Congress depict: (Circle one)

a) Mahommed and his prophet
b) Confucius and his scribe
c) Moses (Old Testament) and Paul the Apostle (New Testament) of the Bible.
d) Zeus and Apollo

xiv) What does the above tell you about the Religion of America? America is: (Circle one)

a) An atheistic nation
b) A Buddhist nation
c) A Christian nation
d) An Islamic nation

xv) In the Main Reading Room of the Library of Congress Thomas Jefferson building, whom does the statue representing *History* extol? (Circle one)

    a) Marco Polo
    b) William the Conqueror
    c) Alexander the Great
    d) Almighty God of the Bible

xvi) Why is the old historic 1897 Library of Congress building called *The Thomas Jefferson building*? (Fill in the blanks)

    a) The old historic 1897 Library of Congress building is called the *Thomas Jefferson building*, because Thomas Jefferson_____ _____ his own personal _____ to_____, consisting of_____ priceless volumes at Congress' own price, to _____ for the_____ _____ of the_____.

xvii) In the inner dome of the Main Reading Room of the Library of Congress, *Religion* is Judea's contribution to the world. Judea is represented as: (Fill in the blanks)

    a) An _____ woman, her_____ raised in _____ and _____ to _____ _____. The_____ _____ stand at her_____; the scroll of the_____ _____ on her lap.

2. Christian Character Traits:

Select 10 Christian character traits exemplified in the art, inscriptions, sculpture and architecture of our national 1897 Library of Congress, Thomas Jefferson building. List them below:

a. _____   f. _____

b. _____   g. _____

c. _____   h. _____

d. _____   i. _____

e. _____   j. _____

IV. *Illustrate your work with pictures, outline map, models and drawings.*

V. *Memory verse:*

What doth the Lord require of thee, but to do justly, to love mercy and to walk humbly with thy God? (Micah 6:8)

The White House – 1600 Pennsylvania Avenue

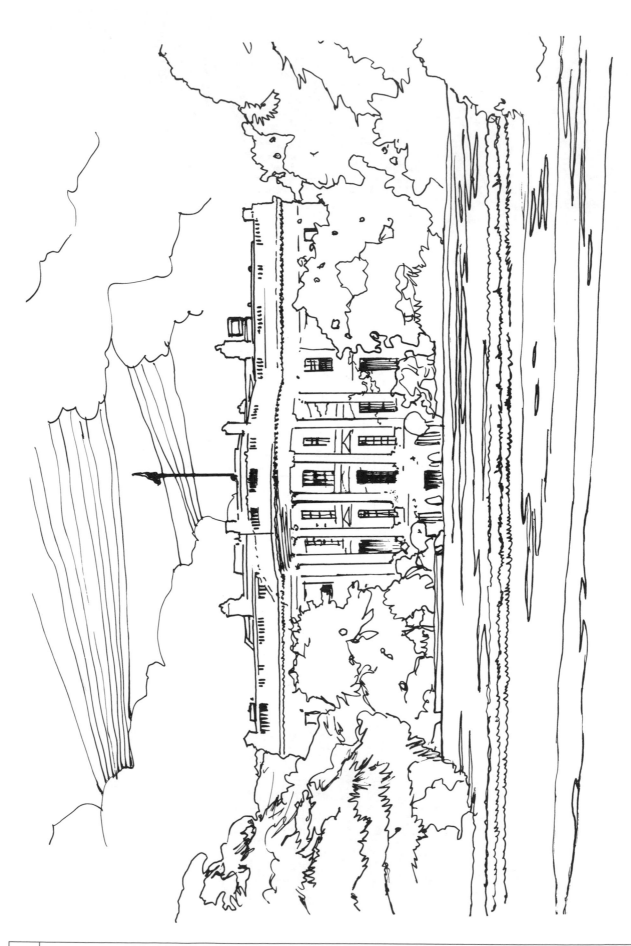

The White House – South Façade

The Christian Heritage Of Our Nation - History Curriculum

After Gilbert Stuart's Famed 1796 Painting of George Washington
– East Room of the White House –

I Pray Heaven To Bestow THE BEST OF BLESSINGS ON THIS HOUSE And All that shall hereafter Inhabit it May none but Honest and Wise Men ever rule under This Roof.

November MDCCC

From a Letter of JOHN ADAMS

The White House State Dining Room Mantel.

From the Original Portrait by Gilbert Stuart
Made While Washington was a Regular
Attendant at Christ Church.
Handbook of Christ Church, Philadelphia, 1920

George Washington's Sunday Morning Prayer

The Christian Heritage Of Our Nation - History Curriculum

...ed, that I may not do mine own works, but wait on thee, and discharge those weighty duties thou requirest of me; and since thou art a God of pure eyes, and wilt be sanctified in all who draw near unto thee, who dost not regard the sacrifice of fools, nor hear sinners who tread in thy courts, pardon I beseech thee, my sins, remove them from thy presence, as far as the east is from the west, and accept of me for the merits of thy son Jesus Christ, that when I come into thy temple, and compass thine altar, my prayers may come before thee as incense, and as I desire thou wouldst hear me calling upon thee in my prayer, so give me grace to hear thee calling on me in thy word, that...

George Washington's Sunday Morning Prayer

A may be wisdom, righteousness
reconciliation & peace to the
saving of my soul in the day
of the Lord Jesus. Grant that
I hear it with reverence
I may ~~~~ ~~~~~~~~~~~
receive it with meekness, min-
-gle it with faith, and that
it may accomplish in me, Gracious God, the good work for which
thou hast sent it. Bless my
family, kindred, friends, and
country, be our God & guide
this day and for ever for his
sake., lay down in the Grave
and arose again for us, Jesus
Christ our Lord. Amen.

_____

Sunday evening.
O most glorious God, in Jesus
Christ my merciful & loving
Father, I acknowledge and
confess the guilt, in the weak

George Washington's Sunday Evening Prayer

and imperfect performance
of the duties of this day.
I have called on thee for pardon and forgiveness of sins,
but so coldly & carelessly, that
my prayers are become my sin
and stand in need of pardon
I have heard thy holy word, but
with such deadness of spirit
that I have been an unprofitable and forgetful hearer, so
that O Lord, tho' I have done thy work
yet it hath been so negligent
that I may rather expect a
curse than a blessing from thee
But O God, who art rich in mercy
and plenteous in redemption,
mark not I beseech thee what
I have done amiss, remember

George Washington's Sunday Evening Prayer

[from that book, and remit my transgressions, negligences, & ignorances, and cover them all with the absolute obedience of thy dear Son, that those sacrifices which I have offered may be accepted by thee, in and for the sacrifice of Jesus Christ offered upon the cross for me; for his sake, ease me of the burden of my sins, and give me grace that by the call of the Gospel I may rise from the slumber of sin into newness of life. Let me live according to those holy rules which Thou hast this day prescribed in thy holy word. Make me to know what is acceptable in thy sight, and therein to delight. Open the eyes of my under-]

George Washington's Sunday Evening Prayer

standing, and help me thoroughly to examine myself concerning my knowledge, faith, and repentance. increase my faith, and direct me to the true object Jesus Christ the way, the truth, and the life. bless O Lord all the people of this land, from the highest to the lowest, particularly those whom thou hast appointed to rule as in church & state, continue thy goodness to me this night. These weak petitions so humbly implore thee to hear accept & ans for the sake of thy Dear Son Jesus Christ our Lord. amen

_____

Monday morning
O Eternal, and everlasting God, I presume to present myself this morning before thy divine majesty, beseeching thee to accept of my hum

George Washington's Sunday Evening Prayer

LESSON 5

THE WHITE HOUSE - EXECUTIVE BRANCH OF OUR GOVERNMENT

I Pray Heaven to Bestow the best of Blessings on this House and all that shall hereafter inhabit it. May none but Honest and Wise Men ever rule under this Roof.

John Adams, President, United States of America[29]

Of all the public buildings in the new capital city, the cornerstone for the President's House was the first to be laid. This took place in 1792. L'Enfant's original three-point plan incorporated the President's House, executive branch of our government, the Capitol, its legislative branch, and a monument in honor of George Washington, first President of the United States.

Of the designs submitted for this mansion which was to accommodate the first officer of the United States and his family, one was by a mysterious Mr. A.Z., later known to be Thomas Jefferson; another by a certain James Diamond of Somerset County, Maryland, and one by James Hoban, Irishman born in County Kilkenny, Ireland.[30] Hoban received an award for his design which won the competition sponsored by the commissioners of the District of Columbia.[31]

The north facade of this spacious mansion is said to resemble Leinster House in Dublin, Ireland. It is constructed of sandstone from Aquia Creek in Virginia and now comprises 132 rooms and 20 baths. The south facade of the mansion resembles the Chateau de Rastignac in the Perigord, France.[32] The design is Palladian in style and comes from the famous Italian architect, Andrea Palladio.[33]

The magnificent south balcony is where Heads of State are received by the President of the United States, and where they deliver their public addresses to a large crowd assembled on the South Lawn during official state visits. An inspection of the military guard ensues, while the Marine Corps band adds color, music and pageantry to this splendid tradition.

The President's helicopter alights on the South Lawn.

The first President to occupy this home was John Adams, second President of the United States. When Adams first arrived at his new residence on November 1, 1800, he penned these words to his wife, Abigail:

I pray heaven to bestow the best of blessings on this House, and all that shall hereafter inhabit it. May none but honest and wise men ever rule under this roof.

The Christian Heritage Of Our Nation - History Curriculum

His magnificent prayer was carved into the State Dining Room mantel by President Franklin Delano Roosevelt, many years later.

Shortly after she arrived at the President's House to join her husband, Abigail Adams poured out her heart to her daughter, describing her new surroundings:

> Not one room or chamber is finished of the whole. It is habitable by fires in every part, thirteen of which we are obliged to keep daily or sleep in wet and damp places. To assist us in this great castle, and render less attendance necessary, bells are wholly wanting and promises are all you can obtain. This is so great an inconvenience that I know not what to do. . .We have not the least fence, yard or other convenience, without, and the great unfinished audience room (East Room) I make a drying room of, to hang up the clothes in.[34]

Abigail made the best of her new role as First Lady, however, adding:

> You must keep all this to yourself, and when asked how I like it, say that I write you the situation is beautiful, which is true. . .It is a beautiful spot, capable of every improvement, and the more I view it, the more I am delighted with it.[35]

Today, the East Room is the largest room in the White House and is used for State balls, receptions, press conferences, and many other special events. Several weddings have occurred in this beautiful room, to include those of Nellie Grant, Alice Roosevelt and Lynda Bird Johnson. This was also the historic scene of funeral services for Presidents William Henry Harrison, Zachary Taylor, Abraham Lincoln, Warren G. Harding, and Franklin Delano Roosevelt. Displayed here is the most distinguished portrait in the house, that of George Washington painted by Gilbert Stuart. Dolley Madison had the foresight and presence of mind to have the canvas taken out of its frame and moved to safety during the 1812-1814 war, when the British set fire to all the public buildings in Washington.[36] Afterwards, in order to camouflage the charred walls, the house was repainted white. It was only in 1905, however, that the mansion gained its new, official name: *The White House.*[37]

Facing the north entrance, a white corridor serves to connect the main part of the mansion with the President's Oval Office from where he makes his appearances on television. To the right of the Oval Office is the Old Executive Office Building, which serves the administrative needs of the White House together with the New Executive Office Building a block away.

Each Christmas marks the anniversary of the *Pageant of Peace*, begun by President Calvin Coolidge. The ceremonies commence with a lighting of the National Christmas tree, a lovely Colorado blue spruce, which directly faces the White House South Lawn from its location on the north side of the Ellipse.[38] Each year, fifty smaller trees form a wide semi-circle on either side, one for each state in the Union. Since 1923 almost every President of the United States has been involved in these ceremonies.[39] Winston Churchill participated in the joyful event of 1941, while visiting Washington after Pearl Harbor. President Harry Truman lit the tree by remote control switch from his native Missouri.[40]

Of further interest to Americans, are George Washington's hand-calligraphied prayers entitled *The Daily Sacrifice* constituting a morning and evening prayer for each day of the week. Following are a number of these, reprinted for all to read:

THE DAILY SACRIFICE

Sunday Morning

ALMIGHTY GOD, and most merciful father, who didst command the children of Israel to offer a daily sacrifice to thee, that thereby they might glorify and praise thee for thy protection both night and day; receive, O Lord, my morning sacrifice which I now offer up to thee; I yield thee humble and hearty thanks that thou hast preserved me from the dangers of the night past, and brought me to the light of this day, and the comforts thereof, a day which is consecrated to thine own service and for thine own honour. Let my heart, therefore, gracious God, be so affected with the glory and majesty of it, that I may not do mine own works, but wait on thee, and discharge those weighty duties thou requirest of me; and since thou art a God of pure eyes, and wilt be sanctified in all who draw near unto thee, who dost not regard the sacrifice of fools, nor hear sinners who tread in thy courts, pardon, I beseech thee my sins, remove them from thy presence as far as the east is from the west, and accept of me for the merits of thy son Jesus Christ, that when I come into thy temple, and compass thine altar my prayer may come before thee as incense and as I desire thou wouldst hear me calling upon thee in my prayers, so give me grace to hear thee calling on me in thy word, that it may be wisdom, righteousness, reconciliation & peace to the saving of my soul in the day of the Lord Jesus. Grant that I may hear it with reverence, receive it with meekness, mingle it with faith, and that it may accomplish in me, gracious God, the good work for which thou hast sent it. Bless my family, kindred, friends and country, be our God & guide this day and for ever for his sake, who lay down in the grave and arose again for us, Jesus Christ our Lord. Amen.

Sunday Evening

O MOST GLORIOUS GOD, in Jesus Christ my merciful & loving father, I acknowledge and confess my guilt, in the weak and imperfect performance of the duties of this day. I have called on thee for pardon and forgiveness of sins, but so coldly & carelessly, that my prayers are become my sin and stand in need of pardon. I have heard thy holy word, but with such deadness of spirit that I have been an unprofitable and forgetful hearer, so that, O Lord, tho' I have done thy work, yet it hath been so negligently that I may rather expect a curse than a blessing from thee. But, O God, who art rich in mercy and plenteous in redemption, mark not, I beseech thee, what I have done amiss; remember I am but dust, and remit my transgressions, negligences & ignorances, and cover them all with the absolute obedience of thy dear Son, that those sacrifices which I have offered may be accepted by thee, in and for the sacrifice Jesus Christ offered upon the cross for me; for his sake, ease me of the burden of my sins, and give me grace that by the call of the Gospel I may rise from the slumber of sin unto newness of life. Let me live according to those holy rules which thou hast this day prescribed in thy holy word; make me to know what is acceptable in thy sight and therein to delight. Open the eyes of my understanding, and help me thoroughly to examine myself concerning my knowledge, faith and repentance. Increase my faith, and direct me to the true object, Jesus Christ the way, the truth and the life. Bless, O Lord, all the people of this land, from the highest to the lowest, particularly those whom thou hast appointed to rule over us in church & state. Continue thy goodness to me this night. These weak petitions I humbly implore thee to hear, accept and answer for the sake of thy Dear Son Jesus Christ our Lord. Amen.

Monday Morning

O ETERNAL AND EVERLASTING GOD, I presume to present myself this morning before thy Divine majesty, beseeching thee to accept of my humble and hearty thanks, that it hath pleased thy great goodness to keep and preserve me the night past from all the dangers poor mortals are subject to, and hast given me sweet and pleasant sleep, whereby I find my body refreshed and comforted for performing the duties of this day, in which I beseech thee to defend me from all perils of body & soul. Direct my thoughts, words and work, wash away my sins in the immaculate blood of the Lamb, and purge my heart by thy Holy Spirit, from the dross of my natural corruption, that I may with more freedom of mind and liberty of will serve thee, the ever living God, in righteousness and holiness this day, and all the days of my life. Increase my faith in the sweet promises of the gospel; give me repentance from dead works; pardon my wanderings, & direct my thoughts unto thyself, the God of my salvation. Teach me how to live in thy fear, labour in thy service, and ever to run in the ways of thy commandments. Make me always watchful over my heart, that neither the terrors of conscience, the loathing of holy duties, the love of sin, nor an unwillingness to depart this life, may cast me into a spiritual slumber, but daily frame me more & more into the likeness of thy son Jesus Christ, that living in thy fear, and dying in thy favour, I may in thy appointed time attain the resurrection of the just unto eternal life. Bless my family, friends & kindred. Unite us all in praising & glorifying thee in all our works begun, continued and ended when we shall come to make our last account before thee blessed Saviour, who hath taught us thus to pray our Father, &c.

MOST GRACIOUS LORD GOD, from whom proceedeth every good and perfect gift, I offer to thy divine majesty my unfeigned praise & thanksgiving for all thy mercies towards me. Thou mad'st me at first and hast ever since sustained the work of thy own hand; thou gav'st thy Son to die for me; and hast given me assurance of salvation, upon my repentance and sincerely endeavouring to conform my life to his holy precepts and example. Thou art pleased to lengthen out to me the time of repentance, and to move me to it by thy spirit and by thy word, by thy mercies, and by thy judgments. Out of a deepness of thy mercies, and my own unworthiness, I do appear before thee at this time; I have sinned and done very wickedly, be merciful to me, O God, and pardon me for Jesus Christ's sake: instruct me in the particulars of my duty, and suffer me not to be tempted above what thou givest me strength to bear. Take care, I pray thee of my affairs and more and more direct me in thy truth. Defend me from my enemies, especially my spiritual ones. Suffer me not to be drawn from thee, by the blandishments of the world, carnal desires, the cunning of the devil, or deceitfulness of sin. Work in me thy good will and pleasure, and discharge my mind from all things that are displeasing to thee, of all ill will and discontent, wrath and bitterness, pride & vain conceit of myself, and render me charitable, pure, holy, patient and heavenly minded. Be with me at the hour of death; dispose me for it, and deliver me from the slavish fear of it, and make me willing and fit to die whenever thou shalt call me hence. Bless our rulers in church and state. Bless O Lord the whole race of mankind, and let the world be filled with the knowledge of Thee and thy son Jesus Christ. Pity the sick, the poor, the weak, the needy, the widows and fatherless, and all that mourn or are broken in heart, and be merciful to them according to their several necessities. Bless my friends and grant me grace to forgive my enemies as heartily as I desire forgiveness of Thee my heavenly Father. I beseech thee to defend me this night from all evil, and do more for me than I can think or ask, for Jesus Christ's sake, in whose most holy name & words, I continue to pray, Our Father, &c.

Tuesday Morning

O LORD OUR GOD, most mighty and merciful father, I thine unworthy creature and servant, do once more approach thy presence. Though not worthy to appear before thee, because of my natural corruptions, and the many sins and transgressions which I have committed against thy divine majesty; yet I beseech thee, for the sake of him in whom thou art well pleased, the Lord Jesus Christ, to admit me to render thee deserved thanks and praises for thy manifold mercies extended toward me, for the quiet rest & repose of the past night, for food, raiment, health, peace, liberty and the hopes of a better life through the merit of thy dear son's bitter passion. And O kind father continue thy mercy and favour to me this day, and ever hereafter; prosper all my lawful undertakings; let me have all my directions from thy holy spirit, and success from thy bountiful hand. Let the bright beams of thy light so shine into my heart, and enlighten my mind in understanding thy blessed word, that I may be enabled to perform thy will in all things, and effectually resist all temptations of the world, the flesh, and the devil. Preserve and defend our rulers in church & state. Bless the people of this land, be a Father to the fatherless, a comforter to the comfortless, a deliverer to the captives, and a physician to the sick. Let thy blessing be upon our friends, kindred and families. Be our guide this day and forever through Jesus Christ, in whose blessed form of prayer I conclude my weak petitions—Our Father, &c.

Tuesday Evening

MOST GRACIOUS GOD and heavenly father, we cannot cease, but must cry unto thee for mercy, because my sins cry against me for justice. How shall I address myself unto thee. I must with the publican stand and admire at thy great goodness, tender mercy, and long suffering towards me, in that thou hast kept me the past day from being consumed and brought to nought. O Lord, what is man, or the son or man, that thou regardest him; the more days pass over my head, the more sins and iniquities I heap up against thee. If I should cast up the account of my good deeds done this day, how few and small would they be; but if I should reckon my miscarriages, surely they would be many and great. O blessed Father, let thy son's blood wash me from all impurities, and cleanse me from the stains of sin that are upon me. Give me grace to lay hold upon his merits; that they may be my reconciliation and atonement unto thee.—That I may know my sins are forgiven by his death & passion. Embrace me in the arms of thy mercy; vouchsafe to receive me into the bosom of thy love. Shadow me with thy wings, that I may safely rest under thy protection this night; and so into thy hands I commend myself, both soul & body, in the name of thy son Jesus Christ beseeching Thee, when this life shall end, I may take my everlasting rest with thee in thy heavenly kingdom. Bless all in authority over us, be merciful to all those afflicted with any cross or calamity. Bless all my friends, forgive my enemies and accept of my thanksgiving this evening for all the mercies and favours afforded me; hear and graciously answer these my requests, and whatever else thou see'st needful grant us, for the sake of Jesus Christ in whose blessed name and words I continue to pray, Our Father, &c.

Wednesday Morning

ALMIGHTY AND ETERNAL LORD GOD, the great creator of heaven & earth, and the God and Father of our Lord Jesus Christ; look down from heaven, in pity and compassion upon me thy servant, who humbly prostrate myself before thee, sensible of thy mercy and my own misery; there is an infinite distance between thy glorious majesty and me, thy poor creature, the work of thy hand, between thy infinite power, and my weakness, thy wisdom, and my folly, thy eternal Being, and my mortal frame, but, O Lord, I have set myself at a greater distance from thee by my sin and wickedness, and humbly acknowledge the corruption of my nature and the many rebellions of my life. I have sinned against heaven and before thee, in thought, word & deed; I have contemned thy majesty and holy laws. I have likewise sinned by omitting what I ought to have done, and committing what I ought not. I have rebelled against light, despised thy mercies and judgments, and broken my vows and promises; I have neglected the means of grace, and opportunities of becoming better; my iniquities are multiplied, and my sins are very great. I confess them, O Lord, with shame and sorrow, detestation and loathing, and desire to be vile in my own eyes, as I have rendered myself vile in thine. I humbly beseech thee to be merciful to me in the free pardon of my sins, for the sake of thy dear Son, my only saviour, Jesus Christ, who came not to call the righteous, but sinners to repentance; be pleased to renew my nature, and write thy laws upon my heart, and help me to live righteously, soberly and godly in this evil world; make me humble, meek, patient and contented, and work in me the grace of thy Holy Spirit. Prepare me for death and judgment, and let the thoughts thereof awaken me to a greater care and study to approve myself unto thee in well doing. Bless our rulers in church & state. Help all in affliction or adversity—give them patience and a sanctified use of their affliction, and in thy good time deliverance from them: forgive my enemies, take me into thy protection this day, keep me in perfect peace, which I ask in the name & for the sake of Jesus. Amen.

Wednesday Evening

HOLY AND ETERNAL LORD GOD who art the King of heaven, and the watchman of Israel, that never slumberest or sleepest, what shall we render unto thee for all thy benefits: because thou hast inclined thine ear unto me, therefore will I call on thee as long as I live, from the rising of the sun to the going down of the same let thy name be praised. Among the infinite riches of thy mercy towards me, I desire to render thanks & praise for thy merciful preservation of me this day, as well as all the days of my life; and for the many other blessings & mercies spiritual & temporal which thou hast bestowed on me, contrary to my deserving. All these thy mercies call on me to be thankful and my infirmities & wants call for a continuance of thy tender mercies: cleanse my soul, O Lord, I beseech thee, from whatever is offensive to thee, and hurtful to me, and give me what is convenient for me. Watch over me this night, and give me comfortable and sweet sleep to fit me for the service of the day following. Let my soul watch for the coming of the Lord Jesus; let my bed put me in mind of my grave, and my rising from there of my last resurrection; O heavenly Father, so frame this heart of mine, that I may ever delight to live according to thy will and command, in holiness and righteousness before thee all the days of my life. Let me remember, O Lord, the time will come when the trumpet shall sound, and the dead shall arise and stand before the judgment seat, and give an account of whatever they have done in the body, and let me so prepare my soul, that I may do it with joy and not with grief. Bless the rulers and people of this land and forget not those who are under any affliction or oppression. Let thy favour be extended to all my relations, friends and all others who I ought to remember in my prayers and hear me I beseech thee for the sake of my dear redeemer in whose most holy words, I farther pray, Our Father, &c.[41]

Perhaps the most revealing — and certainly the most intimate sketch of Washington's life and character, is that penned by his own pastor and biographer, the Reverend Mason L. Weems, in 1800. Housed in the Rare Book Collection of the Library of Congress, this unique historical account begins with a dedication to

Martha Washington, *the Illustrious Relict of General George Washington*:

Very Honored Madam,

The author hopes he shall escape the charge of presumption for dedicating this little book to you, as it treats of one, to whom, you, of all on earth, were, and still are, the most tenderly related. One of my reasons for writing this sketch of your husband's life and virtues, is derived from those virtues themselves, which are such true brilliants as to assure me, that even in my simple style, like diamonds on the earth, they will so play their part at sparkling, that many an honest youth shall long to place them in the casket of his own bosom. Should it contribute, in any wise, to diffuse the spirit of Washington - in any degree to promote those virtues, which rendered him the greatest, because the most serviceable of mankind. Should it serve to soothe the sorrows of Washington's dear Relict, during her short separation from that best of husbands, how brightest of saints. And O! Should it be so favoured as to suggest to the children, now that their father is dead, the great duty of burying their quarrels, and of heartily being united to love, and to promote each other's good; it will be matter of great joy to one, who can sincerely subscribe himself the lover of all, who, fear God, honor the President (Adams and Jefferson), revere the laws, and are not given to change. May God's everlasting consolations attend the bosom friend of Washington, is the prayer of orphan'd America; and the prayer of, Honored Madam,

Your sincere. . .friend
M.L.Weems

February 22nd, 1800.

It continues as follows:

The Life of George Washington, Esq.

This truly great man, the third son of Mr. Augustin Washington, was born in Westmoreland County, Virginia on the 22nd day of February, 1732. He was the first son of a second marriage; a circumstance which ought, in all conscience, to quiet the minds of those who have their doubts in respect to the lawfulness of second marriages. His education was of the private and proper sort. Dead languages, pride and pedantry, had no charms for him who always preferred sense to sound, the kernel to the shell. A grammatical knowledge of his mother tongue, the mathematics, geography, history, natural and moral philosophy, were the valuable objects of his youthful studies: And in these he made the proficiency of one who always loved to go deep. At school he was remarkable for good nature and candour; qualities which acquired him so entirely the hearts of his young companions, that a reference to him was the usual mode of deciding all differences. After leaving his tutor he acted for a few years, as a county surveyor, in which profession, his industry, as also the neatness and regularity with which he did everything, were universally admired.

In 1753, the French and Indians began to make inroads on our western frontiers along the Ohio. Governor Dinwiddie was very desirous to get a letter of remonstrance to their Commander in Chief. He had applied, to several young gentlemen of his acquaintance; but they were all so exceedingly tender of their night-caps, that they could not be prevailed on, for love or money, to venture out among the savages. Washington happening to hear of it, instantly waited on his excellency, and offered his services, but not without being terribly afraid lest his want of a beard should go against him. However, the Governor was so charmed with his modesty and manly air, that he never asked him a syllable about his age, but, after thanking him for 'a noble youth,' and insisting on his taking a glass of wine with him, slipped a commission into his hand. The next day, accompanied by an interpreter and a couple of servants, he set out on his expedition, which was, from start to pole, as disagreeable and dangerous as anything Hercules himself could have wished. Soaking rains, chilling blasts, roaring floods, pathless woods, and the mountains clad in snows opposed his course; but opposed in vain. The glorious ambition to serve his country imparted an animation to his nerves, which rendered him superior to all difficulties, and happier far than the little souls he left behind in Williamsburg, carousing and card-playing in the Rawleigh.* Returning homewards, he was waylaid and shot at by a French Indian, and though the copper-coloured ruffian was not 15 steps distant when he fired at him, yet not even so much as the smell of lead passed on the clothes of our young hero; so true still is the promise on record in the good old book, viz. "The hosts of God encamp around the dwellings of the just; And mighty angels wait on all, who in His mercy trust."

On his return to Williamsburg, it was found that he had executed his negociations, both with the French and Indians, with so much fidelity and judgment, that he received that heartfelt thanks of the Governor and Council for the very important services he had done his country. . .He was now (in the 20th year of his age) appointed major and adjutant-general of the Virginia forces. Soon after this, the French continuing their encroachments, orders were given by the English government for the colonies to arm and unite in one confederacy. Virginia took the lead, and raised a regiment of 400 men, at the head of which she placed her darling Washington. With this handful of brave fellows, Col. Washington, not yet 23, boldly pushed out into the Indian country and there, for a considerable time, Hannibal-like, maintained the war against three times the number of French and Indians. . .Hence one of his European friends advised him to quit a scene of danger to which he had such slender ties, and fly with him to the safe and pleasant shores of Europe. "What, replied Washington, shall I forsake my Mother, because she is in danger?" The other observed that Col. Washington had not perhaps duly appreciated the pleasures he was renouncing, the dangers he was incurring. "God forbid," rejoined Washington, "that I should ever appreciate pleasure, opposite to duty, or shrink from dangers when my country calls. No! I had rather suffer with her, than reign with her oppressors." His conduct was agreeable to his principles. In the ever memorable 1775, he embraced his weeping consort, and went forth to Leonidas of his country resolving to fix

*Note: A famous tavern in Williamsburg, christened *Rawleigh*, in honor I suppose, of the great Sir Walter.

The Christian Heritage Of Our Nation - History Curriculum

her liberties or find a glorious grave. For seven long years he kept the fields of iron war, with no dainties, but common soldiers' fare; no music but clashing arms and thundering guns; no pleasures, but his toils and watching for us. At any period of this long conflict, he might no doubt, have exchanged our liberties for myriads of shining gold, or highest feats of purpled honor. But Washington was not born to blast the hope of millions, or bid the genius of his country hang her head and weep. . .[42]

Washington's Addresses to the Churches

On April 30, 1789, George Washington was sworn into office as first president with his left hand upon the Bible, opened to Genesis, Chapter 49-50. Genesis 49:22-25c, upon which his hand lay, was Washington's inaugural Scripture. He swore allegiance to the U.S. Constitution with his right hand upraised, the event taking place in Federal Hall, New York. As first president of the United States, George Washington received letters of congratulations from fourteen churches. In response, he penned the following personal addresses:

TO THE MINISTERS, CHURCH-WARDENS, AND VESTRY-MEN OF THE GERMAN LUTHERAN CONGREGATION, IN AND NEAR THE CITY OF PHILADELPHIA.

April 20th, 1789

Gentlemen,

While I request you to accept my thanks for your kind address, I must profess myself highly gratified by the sentiments of esteem and consideration contained in it. The approbation my past conduct has received from so worthy a body of citizens as that, whose joy for my appointment you announce, is a proof of the indulgence with which my future transactions will be judged by them.

I could not, however, avoid apprehending, that the partiality of my countrymen in favor of the measures now pursued, had led them to expect too much from the present government, did not the same Providence, which has been visible in every stage of our progress to this interesting crisis, from a combination of circumstances, give us cause to hope for the accomplishment of all our reasonable desires.

Thus partaking with you in the pleasing anticipation of the blessings of a wise and efficient government, I flatter myself that opportunities will not be wanting for me to show my disposition to encourage the domestic and public virtues of industry, economy, patriotism, philanthropy, and that righteousness which exalteth a nation.

I rejoice in having so suitable an occasion to testify the reciprocity of my esteem for the numerous people whom you represent. From the excellent character for diligence, sobriety, and virtue, which the Germans in general, who are settled in America, have ever maintained, I cannot forbear felicitating myself on receiving from so respectable a number of them such strong assurances of their affection for my person, confidence in my integrity, and zeal to support me in my endeavours for promoting the welfare of our common country.

So long as my conduct shall merit the approbation of the wise and the good, I hope to hold the same place in your affections, which your friendly declarations induce me to believe I possess at present; and, amidst all the vicissitudes, that may await me in this mutable existence, I shall earnestly desire the continuation of an interest in your intercession at the throne of grace.

GEORGE WASHINGTON

TO THE GENERAL ASSEMBLY OF THE PRESBYTERIAN CHURCH IN THE UNITED STATES.

May, 1789

Gentlemen,

I receive with great sensibility the testimonial given by the General Assembly of the Presbyterian Church in the United States of America, of the lively and unfeigned pleasure experienced by them on my appointment to the first office in the nation.

Although it will be my endeavour to avoid being elated by the too favorable opinion, which your kindness for me may have induced you to express of the importance of my former conduct and the effect of my future services, yet, conscious of the disinterestedness of my motives, it is not necessary for me to conceal the satisfaction I have felt upon finding, that my compliance with the call of my country, and my dependence on the assistance of Heaven to support me in my arduous undertakings, have, so far as I can learn, met the universal approbation of my countrymen.

While I reiterate the professions of my dependence upon Heaven, as the source of all public and private blessings, I will observe, that the general prevalence of piety, philanthropy, honesty, industry, and economy seems, in the ordinary course of human affairs, particularly necessary for advancing and confirming the happiness of our country. While all men within our territories are protected in worshipping the Deity according to the dictates of their consciences, it is rationally to be expected from them in return, that they will all be emulous of evincing the sanctity of their professions by the innocence of their lives and the beneficence of their actions; for no man, who is profligate in his morals, or a bad member of the civil community, can possibly be a true Christian, or a credit to his own religious society.

I desire you to accept my acknowledgments for your laudable endeavours to render men sober, honest, and good citizens, and the obedient subjects of a lawful government, as well as for your prayers to Almighty God for his blessing on our common country, and the humble instrument, which he has been pleased to make use of in the administration of its government.

GEORGE WASHINGTON

TO THE BISHOPS OF THE METHODIST EPISCOPAL CHURCH IN THE UNITED STATES.

May, 1789

Gentlemen,

I return to you individually, and, through you, to your society collectively in the United States, my thanks for the demonstrations of affection and the expressions of joy, offered in their behalf, on my late appointment. It shall still be my endeavour to manifest, by overt acts, the purity of my inclinations for promoting the happiness of mankind, as well as the sincerity of my desires to contribute whatever may be in my power towards the preservation of the civil and religious liberties of the American people. In pursuing this line of conduct, I hope, by the assistance of Divine Providence, not altogether to disappoint the confidence, which you have been pleased to repose in me.

It always affords me satisfaction, when I find a concurrence in sentiment and practice between all conscientious men in acknowledgments of homage to the great Governor of the Universe, and in professions of support to a just civil government. After mentioning, that I trust the people of every denomination, who demean themselves as good citizens, will have occasion to be convinced, that I shall always strive to prove a faithful and impartial patron of genuine, vital religion, I must assure you in particular, that I take in the kindest part the promise you make of presenting your prayers at the throne of grace for me, and that I likewise implore the divine benediction of yourselves and your religious community.

GEORGE WASHINGTON

TO THE GENERAL COMMITTEE, REPRESENTING THE UNITED BAPTIST CHURCHES IN VIRGINIA.

May, 1789

Gentlemen,

I request that you will accept my best acknowledgments for your congratulation on my appointment to the first office in the nation. The kind manner in which you mention my past conduct equally claims the expression of my gratitude.

After we had, by the smiles of Heaven on our exertions, obtained the object for which we contended, I retired, at the conclusion of the war, with an idea that my country could have no farther occasion for my services, and with the intention of never entering again into public life; but, when the exigencies of my country seemed to require me once more to engage in public affairs, an honest conviction of duty superseded my former resolution, and became my apology for deviating from the happy plan which I had adopted.

If I could have entertained the slightest apprehension, that the constitution framed in the convention, where I had the honor to preside, might possibly endanger the religious rights of any ecclesiastical society, certainly I would have never placed my signature to it; and, if I could now conceive that the general government might ever be so administered as to render the liberty of conscience insecure, I beg you will be persuaded, that no one would be more zealous than myself to establish effectual barriers against the horrors of spiritual tyranny, and every species of religious persecution. For you doubtless remember, that I have often expressed my sentiments, that every man, conducting himself as a good citizen, and being accountable to God alone for his religious opinions, ought to be protected in worshipping the Deity according to the dictates of his own conscience.

While I recollect with satisfaction, that the religious society of which you are members have been, throughout America, uniformly and almost unanimously the firm friends to civil liberty, and the persevering promoters of our glorious revolution, I cannot hesitate to believe, that they will be the faithful supporters of a free, yet efficient general government. Under this pleasing expectation I rejoice to assure them, that they may rely on my best wishes and endeavours to advance their prosperity.

In the mean time be assured, Gentlemen, that I entertain a proper sense of your fervent supplications to God for my temporal and eternal happiness.

GEORGE WASHINGTON

TO THE MINISTERS AND ELDERS OF THE GERMAN REFORMED CONGREGATIONS IN THE UNITED STATES.

June, 1789

Gentlemen,

I am happy in concurring with you in the sentiments of gratitude and piety towards Almighty God, which are expressed with such fervency of devotion in your address; and in believing, that I shall always find in you, and the German Reformed Congregations in the United States, a conduct correspondent to such worthy and pious expressions.

At the same time, I return you my thanks for the manifestation of your firm purpose to support in your persons a government founded in justice and equity, and for the promise, that it will be your constant study to impress the minds of the people intrusted to your care with a due sense of the necessity of uniting reverence to such a government, and obedience to its laws, with the duties and exercises of religion.

Be assured, Gentlemen, it is by such conduct very much in the power of the virtuous members of the community to alleviate the burden of the important office which I have accepted, and to give me occasion to rejoice, in this world, for having followed therein the dictates of my conscience.

Be pleased, also, to accept my acknowledgments for the interest you so kindly take in the prosperity of my person, family, and administration. May your devotions before the throne of grace be prevalent in calling down the blessings of Heaven upon yourselves and your country.

GEORGE WASHINGTON

TO THE DIRECTORS OF THE SOCIETY OF THE UNITED BRETHREN FOR PROPAGATING THE GOSPEL AMONG THE HEATHEN.

July, 1789

Gentlemen,

I receive with satisfaction the congratulations of your society, and of the Brethren's congregations in the United States of America. For you may be persuaded, that the approbation and good wishes of such a peaceable and virtuous community cannot be indifferent to me.

You will also be pleased to accept my thanks for the treatise* you presented; and be assured of my patronage in your laudable undertakings.

In proportion as the general government of the United States shall acquire strength by duration, it is probable they may have it in their power to extend a salutary influence to the aborigines in the extremities of their territory. In the mean time, it will be a desirable thing, for the protection of the Union, to co-operate, as far as the circumstances may conveniently admit, with the disinterested endeavours of your Society to civilize and christianize the savages of the wilderness.

Under these impressions, I pray Almighty God to have you always in his holy keeping.

GEORGE WASHINGTON

* "An Account of the Manner, in which the Protestant Church of the *Unitas Fratrum,* or United Brethren, preach the Gospel and carry on their Mission among the Heathen."

TO THE BISHOPS, CLERGY, AND LAITY OF THE PROTESTANT EPISCOPAL CHURCH IN THE STATES OF NEW YORK, NEW JERSEY, PENNSYLVANIA, DELAWARE, MARYLAND, VIRGINIA, AND NORTH CAROLINA, IN GENERAL CONVENTION ASSEMBLED.

August 19th, 1789

Gentlemen,

I sincerely thank you for your affectionate congratulations on my election to the chief magistracy of the United States.

After having received from my fellow-citizens in general the most liberal treatment, after having found them disposed to contemplate, in the most flattering point of view, the performance of my military services, and the manner of my retirement at the close of the war, I feel that I have a right to console myself in my present arduous undertakings with a hope, that they will still be inclined to put the most favorable construction on the motives, which may influence me in my future public transactions.

The satisfaction arising from the indulgent opinion entertained by the American people of my conduct will, I trust, be some security for preventing me from doing anything, which might justly incur the forfeiture of that opinion. And the consideration, that human happiness and moral duty are inseparably connected, will always continue to prompt me to promote the progress of the former by inculcating the practice of the latter.

On this occasion, it would ill become me to conceal the joy I have felt in perceiving the fraternal affection, which appears to increase every day among the friends of genuine religion. It affords edifying prospects, indeed, to see Christians of different denominations dwell together in more charity, and conduct themselves in respect to each other with a more Christian-like spirit, than ever they have done in any former age, or in any other nation.

I receive with the greater satisfaction your congratulations on the establishment of the new constitution of government, because I believe its mild yet efficient operations will tend to remove every remaining apprehension of those, with whose opinions it may not entirely coincide, as well as to confirm the hopes of its numerous friends; and because the moderation, patriotism, and wisdom of the present federal legislature seem to promise the restoration of order and our ancient virtues, the extension of genuine religion, and the consequent advancement of our respectability abroad, and of our substantial happiness at home.

I request, most reverend and respected Gentlemen, that you will accept my cordial thanks for your devout supplications to the Supreme Ruler of the Universe in behalf of me. May you, and the people you represent, be the happy subjects of the divine benedictions both here and hereafter.

GEORGE WASHINGTON

TO THE SYNOD OF THE REFORMED DUTCH CHURCH IN NORTH AMERICA.

October, 1789

Gentlemen,

I receive with a grateful heart your pious and affectionate address, and with truth declare to you, that no circumstance of my life has affected me more sensibly, or produced more pleasing emotions, than the friendly congratulations, and strong assurances of support, which I have received from my fellow-citizens of all descriptions upon my election to the Presidency of these United States.

I fear, Gentlemen, your goodness has led you to form too exalted an opinion of my virtues and merits. If such talents as I possess have been called into action by great events, and those events have terminated happily for our country, the glory should be ascribed to the manifest interposition of an overruling Providence. My military services have been abundantly recompensed by the flattering approbation of a grateful people; and if a faithful discharge of my civil duties can insure a like reward, I shall feel myself richly compensated for any personal sacrifice I may have made by engaging again in public life.

The citizens of the United States of America have given as signal a proof of their wisdom and virtue, in framing and adopting a constitution of government without bloodshed or the intervention of force, as they, upon a former occasion, exhibited to the world, of their valor, fortitude, and perseverance; and it must be a pleasing circumstance to every friend of good order and social happiness to find, that our new government is gaining strength and respectability among the citizens of this country, in proportion as its operations are known and its effects felt.

You, Gentlemen, act the part of pious Christians and good citizens by your prayers and exertions to preserve that harmony and good will towards men, which must be the basis of every political establishment; and I readily join with you, that, "while just government protects all in their religious rights, true religion affords to government its surest support."

I am deeply impressed with your good wishes for my present and future happiness, and I beseech the Almighty to take you and yours under his special care.

GEORGE WASHINGTON

TO THE RELIGIOUS SOCIETY CALLED QUAKERS, AT THEIR YEARLY MEETING FOR PENNSYLVANIA, NEW JERSEY, DELAWARE, AND THE WESTERN PART OF MARYLAND AND VIRGINIA.

October, 1789

Gentlemen,

I receive with pleasure your affectionate address, and thank you for the friendly sentiments and good wishes, which you express for the success of my administration and for my personal happiness.

We have reason to rejoice in the prospect, that the present national government, which, by the favor of Divine Providence, was formed by the common counsels and peaceably established with the common consent of the people, will prove a blessing to every denomination of them. To render it such, my best endeavours shall not be wanting.

Government being, among other purposes, instituted to protect the persons and consciences of men from oppression, it certainly is the duty of rulers, not only to abstain from it themselves, but, according to their stations, to prevent it in others.

The liberty enjoyed by the people of these States, of worshipping Almighty God agreeably to their consciences, is not only among the choicest of their *blessings*, but also of their *rights*. While men perform their social duties faithfully, they do all that society or the state can with propriety demand or expect; and remain responsible only to their Maker for the religion, or modes of faith, which they may prefer or profess.

Your principles and conduct are well known to me; and it is doing the people called Quakers no more than justice to say, that (except their declining to share with others the burthen of the common defence) there is no denomination among us, who are more exemplary or useful citizens.

I assure you very explicitly, that in my opinion the conscientious scruples of all men should be treated with great delicacy and tenderness; and it is my wish and desire, that the laws may always be as extensively accommodated to them, as a due regard to the protection and essential interests of the nation may justify and permit.

GEORGE WASHINGTON

TO THE ROMAN CATHOLICS IN THE UNITED STATES.

December, 1789

Gentlemen,

While I now receive with much satisfaction your congratulations on my being called by a unanimous vote to the first station in my country, I cannot but duly notice your politeness in offering an apology for the unavoidable delay. As that delay has given you an opportunity of realizing, instead of anticipating, the benefits of the general government, you will do me the justice to believe, that your testimony to the increase of the public prosperity enhances the pleasure, which I should otherwise have experienced from your affectionate address.

I feel, that my conduct in war and in peace has met with more general approbation, than could reasonably have been expected; and I find myself disposed to consider that fortunate circumstance, in a great degree, resulting from the able support and extraordinary candor of my fellow-citizens of all denominations.

The prospect of national prosperity now before us is truly animating, and ought to excite the exertions of all good men to establish and secure the happiness of their country, in the permanent duration of its freedom and independence. America, under the smiles of divine Providence, the protection of a good government, the cultivation of manners, morals, and piety, can hardly fail of attaining an uncommon degree of eminence in literature, commerce, agriculture, improvements at home, and respectability abroad.

As mankind becomes more liberal, they will be more apt to allow, that all those, who conduct themselves as worthy members of the community, are equally entitled to the protection of civil government. I hope ever to see America among the foremost nations in examples of justice and liberality. And I presume, that your fellow-citizens will not forget the patriotic part, which you took in the accomplishment of their revolution and the establishment of their government, or the important assistance, which they received from a nation in which the Roman Catholic religion is professed.

I thank you, Gentlemen, for your kind concern for me. While my life and health shall continue, in whatever situation I may be, it shall be my constant endeavour to justify the favorable sentiments you are pleased to express of my conduct. And may the members of your society in America, animated alone by the pure spirit of Christianity, and still conducting themselves as the faithful subjects of our free government, enjoy every temporal and spiritual felicity.

GEORGE WASHINGTON

TO THE HEBREW CONGREGATION OF
THE CITY OF SAVANNAH.

May, 1790

Gentlemen,

I thank you, with great sincerity, for your congratulations on my appointment to the office, which I have the honor to hold by the unanimous choice of my fellow-citizens; and especially for the expressions, which you are pleased to use in testifying the confidence, that is reposed in me by your congregation.

As the delay, which has naturally intervened between my election and your address, has afforded an opportunity for appreciating the merits of the federal government, and for communicating your sentiments of its administration, I have rather to express my satisfaction, than regret, at a circumstance, which demonstrates (upon experiment) your attachment to the former, as well as approbation of the latter.

I rejoice, that a spirit of liberality and philanthropy is much more prevalent than it formerly was among the enlightened nations of the earth, and that your brethren will benefit thereby in proportion as it shall become still more extensive. Happily, the people of the United States of America have, in many instances, exhibited examples worthy of imitation, the salutary influence of which will doubtless extend much farther, if, gratefully enjoying those blessings of peace, which, under the favor of Heaven, have been obtained by fortitude of war, they shall conduct themselves with reverence to the Deity, and charity towards their fellow-creatures.

May the same wonder-working Deity, who long since delivered the Hebrews from their Egyptian oppressors, and planted them in the promised land, whose providential agency has lately been conspicuous in establishing these United States as an independent nation, still continue to water them with the dews of Heaven, and to make the inhabitants of every denomination participate in the temporal and spiritual blessings of that people, whose God is Jehovah.

GEORGE WASHINGTON

TO THE CONVENTION OF THE UNIVERSAL CHURCH LATELY ASSEMBLED IN PHILADELPHIA.

1790

Gentlemen,

I thank you cordially for the congratulations, which you offer on my appointment to the office I have the honor to hold in the government of the United States.

It gives me the most sensible pleasure to find, that, in our nation, however different are the sentiments of citizens on religious doctrines, they generally concur in one thing; for their political professions and practices are almost universally friendly to the order and happiness of our civil institutions. I am also happy in finding this disposition particularly evinced by your society. It is, moreover, my earnest desire, that all the members of every association or community, throughout the United States, may make such use of the auspicious years of peace, liberty, and free inquiry, with which they are now favored, as they shall hereafter find occasion to rejoice for having done.

With great satisfaction I embrace this opportunity to express my acknowledgments for the interest my affectionate fellow-citizens have taken in my recovery from a late dangerous indisposition; and I assure you, Gentlemen, that, in mentioning my obligations for the effusions of your benevolent wishes in my behalf, I feel animated with new zeal, that my conduct may ever be worthy of your favorable opinion, as well as such as shall, in every respect, best comport with the character of an intelligent and accountable being.

GEORGE WASHINGTON

TO THE CONGREGATIONAL CHURCH AND SOCIETY AT MEDWAY, FORMERLY ST. JOHN'S PARISH, IN THE STATE OF GEORGIA.

May, 1791

Gentlemen,

I learn, with gratitude proportioned to the occasion, your attachment to my person, and the pleasure you express on my election to the Presidency of the United States. Your sentiments on the happy influence of our equal government impress me with the most sensible satisfaction. They vindicate the great interests of humanity; they reflect honor on the liberal minds that entertain them; and they promise the continuance and improvement of that tranquillity, which is essential to the welfare of nations and the happiness of men.

You overrate my best exertions, when you ascribe to them the blessings, which our country so eminently enjoys. From the gallantry and fortitude of her citizens, under the auspices of Heaven, America has derived her independence. To their industry, and the natural advantages of the country, she is indebted for her prosperous situation. From their virtue she may expect long to share the protection of a free and equal government, which their wisdom has established, and which experience justifies, as admirably adapted to our social wants and individual felicity.

Continue, my fellow-citizens, to cultivate the peace and harmony, which now subsist between you and your Indian neighbours. The happy consequence is immediate. The reflection, which arises on justice and benevolence, will be lastingly grateful. A knowledge of your happiness will lighten the cares of my station, and be among the most pleasing of their rewards.

GEORGE WASHINGTON

TO THE MEMBERS OF THE NEW CHURCH IN BALTIMORE.

January, 1793

Gentlemen,

It has ever been my pride to merit the approbation of my fellow-citizens, by a faithful and honest discharge of the duties annexed to those stations, in which they have been pleased to place me; and the dearest rewards of my services have been those testimonies of esteem and confidence, with which they have honored me. But to the manifest interposition of an overruling Providence, and to the patriotic exertions of United America, are to be ascribed those events, which have given us a respectable rank among the nations of the earth.

We have abundant reason to rejoice, that, in this land, the light of truth and reason has triumphed over the power of bigotry and superstition, and that every person may here worship God according to the dictates of his own heart. In this enlightened age, and in this land of equal liberty, it is our boast, that a man's religious tenets will not forfeit the protection of the laws, nor deprive him of the right of attaining and holding the highest offices that are known in the United States.

Your prayers for my present and future felicity are received with gratitude; and I sincerely wish, Gentlemen, that you may in your social and individual capacities taste those blessings, which a gracious God bestows upon the righteous.[43]

GEORGE WASHINGTON

LESSON FIVE

PUPILS' GUIDE

The White House - Executive Branch
of our Government

I. Suggestions for Study

    a)   Read the Lesson material carefully.

    b)   Look up County Kilkenny and Dublin, Ireland; Perigord, France; together with the states of Missouri; Pennsylavania; Delaware; New Jersey; Maryland; Virginia; and North Carolina. Also, the cities of New York, N.Y.; Savannah, GA.; Baltimore, MD.; together with London, England, on your map of the world at home.

II. Lesson Material

    Text: Lesson 5 - The White House, Executive Branch of our Government.

III. 1. *The kind of Nation that America is:*

    i)   Gilbert Stuart's famed portrait of George Washington hangs in the East Room of the White House, because: (Circle one)

        a)   He conquered the British at Yorktown in 1781.

        b)   He laid the cornerstone to the White House in 1792.

        c)   He was the father of our country and the first U.S. president, inaugurated into office.

        d)   He chose the site for the new capital city of the United States of America.

    ii)   What was George Washington's presidential inaugural Scripture upon which his left hand lay, when swearing allegiance to the U.S. Constitution, with his right hand upraised? (Fill in the blanks)

        a)   Joseph is a _____ _____, even a _____ _____ by a well; whose _____ run over a _____: The _____ have sorely _____ him and _____ at him: But his _____ abode in _____, and the _____ of his _____ were made_____ by the_____ of the mighty_____ of Jacob; (from thence is the_____ the _____ of Israel;) Even by the_____ of thy_____, who shall help thee; and by the _____, who shall _____ thee with _____ of _____ above. . .

                        (Verses 22-25c, excerpted from Genesis 49)

iii) This is an unbroken American Christian tradition: All U.S. presidents are sworn into office with their left hand upon the Bible (opened to their Scripture of choice), and with their right hand upraised, swearing allegiance to the U.S. Constitution, praying audibly: "So - help - me - God." (Circle one)

    a) True
    b) False

iv) Where and when was George Washington sworn into office as first U. S. president? (Circle one)

    a) Independence Hall, Philadelphia, January 20, 1789.
    b) Nassau Hall, Princeton, March 5, 1788.
    c) Federal Hall, New York, April 30, 1789.
    d) U.S. Capitol, Washington, D.C., November 5, 1800.

v) List all 14 churches to whom George Washington wrote, thanking them for their letters of congratulations at his inauguration as first U.S. President: (Fill in the blanks)

    a) _____

    b) _____

    c) _____

    d) _____

    e) _____

    f) _____

    g) _____

    h) _____

    i) _____

    j) _____

    k) _____

    l) _____

    m) _____

    n) _____

vi) From the above historical facts, our first president, George Washington, wrote to 13 mainline Christian denominations and one Hebrew synagogue. (Circle one)

   a) False
   b) True

vii) In George Washington's fourth letter of thanks to the churches, addressed to the Baptist churches in Virginia, our first U.S. president states: (Fill in the blanks)

   a) If I could have entertained the slightest _____ that the _____ framed in the_____, where I had the honor to_____, might possibly endanger the_____ rights of any _____ _____, certainly I would never have placed my_____ to it;. . .

viii) In George Washington's fifth letter of thanks to the churches, addressed to the German Reformed Congregations in the United States, our first U.S. president states: (Fill in the blank lines)

   a) . . . May your_____before the_____of_____ be prevalent in calling down the_____ of_____ upon_____ and your_____.

ix) In George Washington's sixth letter of thanks to the churches, addressed to the "Society of the United Brethren for propagating the Gospel among the Heathen," our first U.S. president stated that: (Consult text and fill in the blank lines)

   a) . . . It will be a _____ thing, . . . to cooperate, . . . with the _____ _____ of your Society to _____ and _____ the _____ of the wilderness. Under these impressions, I pray _____ _____ to have you always in His _____ _____.

x) In George Washington's seventh letter of thanks to the churches, addressed to his own Christian denomination, the Protestant Episcopal Church, our first U.S. president states: (Fill in the blanks)

   a) On this_____, it would ill become me to _____ the joy I have felt in _____ the_____ _____, which appears to_____ every day among the friends of_____ _____. It affords edifying_____, indeed, to see_____ of different _____ dwell together in more _____, and conduct themselves in respect to _____ _____ with a more _____ _____,

than ever they have done in any_____ _____ or in any_____
_____.

xi)   George Washington, our first U.S. president, composed his own prayers, comprised of a morning and evening prayer for each day of the week. What title did our first president give to his prayers? (Circle one)

a)   Peace, happiness and prosperity
b)   Brotherly love
c)   The Daily Sacrifice
d)   Successful living

xii) In George Washington's *Sunday Evening Prayer*, our first U.S. president prays in the name of: (Circle one)

a)   A Supreme Being
b)   A universal God
c)   O most glorious God, and Thy dear Son, Jesus Christ our Lord
d)   The Brotherhood of man

xiii) In George Washington's *Sunday Evening Prayer*, our first U.S. president humbly beseeches God to: (Circle all correct answers)

a)   Give him grace to heed the call of the Gospel
b)   Pardon and forgive his sins
c)   Increase his salary
d)   Give him more votes
e)   Remit his transgressions, negligences and ignorances
f)   Cover his sins with the perfect obedience of Jesus Christ

xiv) The above historic evidence proves that George Washington, our first president, unhesitatingly, both in the public and private spheres of his life, confessed his belief in: (Circle one)

a)   Mohammedanism
b)   Buddhism
c)   Deism
d)   Christianity

xv)   The first U.S. president to inhabit the White House was: (Circle one)

a)   George Washington, first U.S. president
b)   John Adams, second U.S. president
c)   Thomas Jefferson, third U.S. president
d)   James Madison, fourth U.S. president

xvi)   When did this event take place? (Circle one)

    a)   November, 1799
    b)   January, 1800
    c)   November, 1800
    d)   January, 1801

xvii)   What beautiful prayer to Almighty God did the first president to inhabit the White House incorporate in a letter to his wife, shortly after arriving? (Fill in the blanks)

    a)   I _____ _____ to _____ the best of _____ on this House and all that shall hereafter _____ it. May none but _____ and _____ men ever rule under this_____.

xviii) Where can this prayer be seen today? This prayer can be seen in: (Circle one)

    a)   The National Archives
    b)   The British Museum
    c)   Engraved upon the mantel of the White House State Dining Room
    d)   Independence Hall, Philadelphia

xix)   From the above, whom did the first U.S. president to inhabit the White House glorify? (Circle one)

    a)   Hammurabi
    b)   Almighty God of the Bible
    c)   Mahommed
    d)   Confucius

2. **Christian character traits:**

Select 10 Christian virtues, values and morals exemplified through the original history and heritage of our first and second U.S. presidents. List them below:

a. _____   f. _____

b. _____   g. _____

c. _____   h. _____

d. _____   i. _____

e. _____   j. _____

IV. Illustrate your work with pictures, outline map, models and drawings.

V. Memory verse: Genesis 49:22-25c

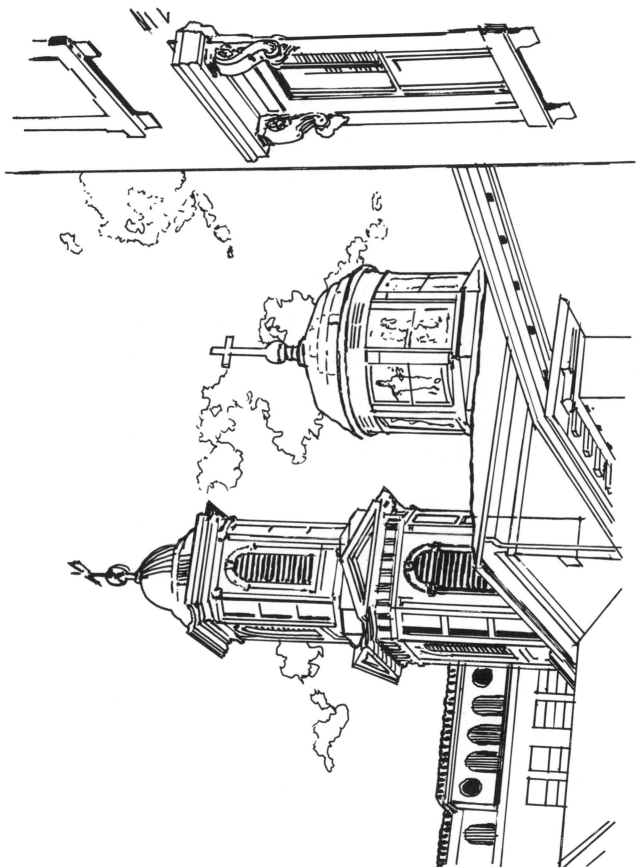

"The Church of the Presidents"

The Resurrection Window, "Church of the Presidents"

The Christian Heritage Of Our Nation - History Curriculum

LESSON 6

THE CHURCH OF THE PRESIDENTS

Across from the White House on "H" Street, N.W., stands St. John's Church on Lafayette Square. Designed in the Greek Revival style by Benjamin Henry Latrobe, one of the architects of the Capitol and foremost architect of his time, this regal little church with its two gilded domes shining in the sun, began its long career of worship services on October 27, 1816. Since its inception, every President of the United States has worshipped the Lord here, some on a more regular basis than others. President Chester Arthur met his wife in this setting. An intimate friend of Dolley Madison, she was a member of the church, and sang in its choir. Here they were married on October 25, 1859, by the Reverend Dr. Pyne, Rector of St. Johns.[44] After her death, President Arthur gave a beautiful stained-glass window entitled *The Resurrection Window* to the church, in loving memory of his wife, Ellen Lewis Herndon Arthur. It faces Lafayette Square and the White House north windows.[45]

Everything within St. John's extols the beauty and glory of God, from its graceful ceilings above to the symbolic windows which capture great truths of our Christian faith. Above the main altar, a stained-glass window shows Christ and his apostles partaking in their last supper together before His crucifixion and triumphant resurrection from the dead. It was designed by Madame Veuve Lorin, curator of stained-glass windows at Chartres Cathedral, France.

St. John's Orphanage

Toward the close of the Civil War, the church Orphanage Association of St. John's Parish sprang up through the loving efforts of St. John's Guild. A ruling of the Guild advised young women that: "One hour every day shall be devoted to the Lord."[46]

The original name of the orphanage was *St. John's Hospital for Children*. It began with a small rented house on Pennsylvania Avenue, in November 1870.[47] The ten beds were promptly filled. A group of five sisters, known as the *Sisterhood of St. John*, soon came into being. Among these, was Sarah Williams Huntington, affectionately known as *Sister Sarah*, who welcomed the poor, sad, rejected and unwanted with open arms. Sister Sarah's mode of operation was "simple living and high thinking."[48]

Records of the early years of this magnificent work of God are non-existent, Sister Sarah having dispensed with "her" children's histories for fear they would jeopardize otherwise promising futures.

A letter and accompanying photograph of the orphans, however, was presented to the President of the Ladies Guild by Mr. Irving M. Grey, alumnus of the orphanage, in

1942. He states that many of the children "made good" in life, one of the boys becoming the Rector of a church in North Carolina. "For this," continues the letter, "so many of us are mighty thankful."[49]

The following excerpted report by Sister Sarah gives an understanding of why she was so beloved, and deeply mourned at her death in 1917:

> We might mention here another case, a most unpromising little waif, brought many years ago by the police, whom we feared to receive lest she should do more harm than receive good. The mother in jail, the most degraded of her class, what could be hoped for the child? But she seemed gradually to forget her old habits, became industrious and useful. At a suitable age she left us for a position which she filled most acceptably, spending her holidays at the orphanage; now the happy wife of an estimable farmer in her own comfortable home. We shudder to think where the little elf might have drifted, had no one held out to her a helping hand.[50]

Now at a different location in our nation's capital, and under different auspices, this ministry begun by the *Church of the Presidents* continues its work among children.

LESSON SIX

PUPILS' GUIDE

"The Church of the Presidents"

I. Suggestions for Study

    a) Read the Lesson material carefully.

    b) Look up Washington, D.C. on your detailed map of the United States at home.

II. Lesson Material

    Text: Lesson 6 - "The Church of the Presidents"

III. 1. The kind of Nation that America is:

    i) Atop the "Church of the Presidents" is prominently displayed: (Circle one)

        a) A weathervane
        b) A compass
        c) The cross of Jesus Christ
        d) Chimes

    ii) President Chester Arthur, 21st president of the United States met his wife, Ellen Lewis Herndon Arthur, at: (Circle one)

        a) A ball
        b) A State Dinner
        c) The races
        d) A Church

    iii) President Chester Arthur's gift to *The Church of the Presidents* teaches the truth about: (Circle one)

        a) The New Deal
        b) The Resurrection of Jesus Christ, our Lord and Savior
        c) Construction
        d) Sports

    iv) What stained-glass window, designed by the curator at *Chartres Cathedral*, France, is featured in predominance in this church? (Consult your text and fill in the blanks)

        a) Above the_____ _____, a stained-glass window shows_____ and His _____partaking in their_____ _____ together

before His _____ and triumphant _____ from the
_____.

v) *The Church of the Presidents,* through the loving efforts of its members, began a Christian work entitled: (Circle one)

    a) Activities and Recreation
    b) Church dinners
    c) Teenage sports programs
    d) St. John's Orphanage

vi) What are some of the fruits of this Christian work: (Consult your text and fill in the blanks)

    a) A 1942 letter from Mr. Irving M. Grey, alumnus of the Orphanage, states that, many of the _____ "_____ _____" in life, one of the _____ becoming the_____ of a _____in North Carolina. "_____ _____," continues the letter, "_____ of us are mighty _____ ."

2. Christian Character Traits:

Select 10 Christian virtues, values and morals woven into the history of *The Church of the Presidents.* List them below:

a. _____   f. _____

b. _____   g. _____

c. _____   h. _____

d. _____   i. _____

e. _____   j. _____

IV. Illustrate your work with pictures, outline map, models and drawings.

V. Memory Verses:

If I speak with the tongues of men and of angels, but do not have love, I have become a noisy gong or a clanging cymbal. . .Love is patient, love is kind, and is not jealous; love does not brag and is not arrogant, does not act unbecomingly; it does not seek its own, is not provoked, does not take into account a wrong suffered, does not rejoice in unrighteousness, but rejoices with the truth; bears all things, believes all things, hopes all things, endures all things. . .But now abide faith, hope, love, these three; but the greatest of these is love.

                     I Corinthians 13:1; 4-7;13

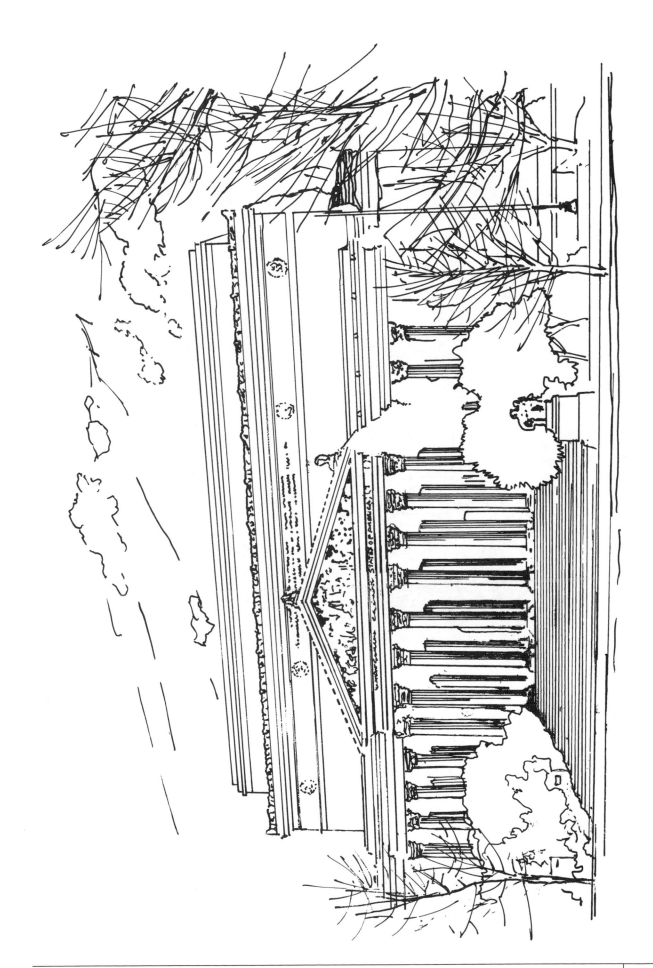

The National Archives – Home of the Declaration of Independence, the U.S. Constitution and the Bill of Rights.

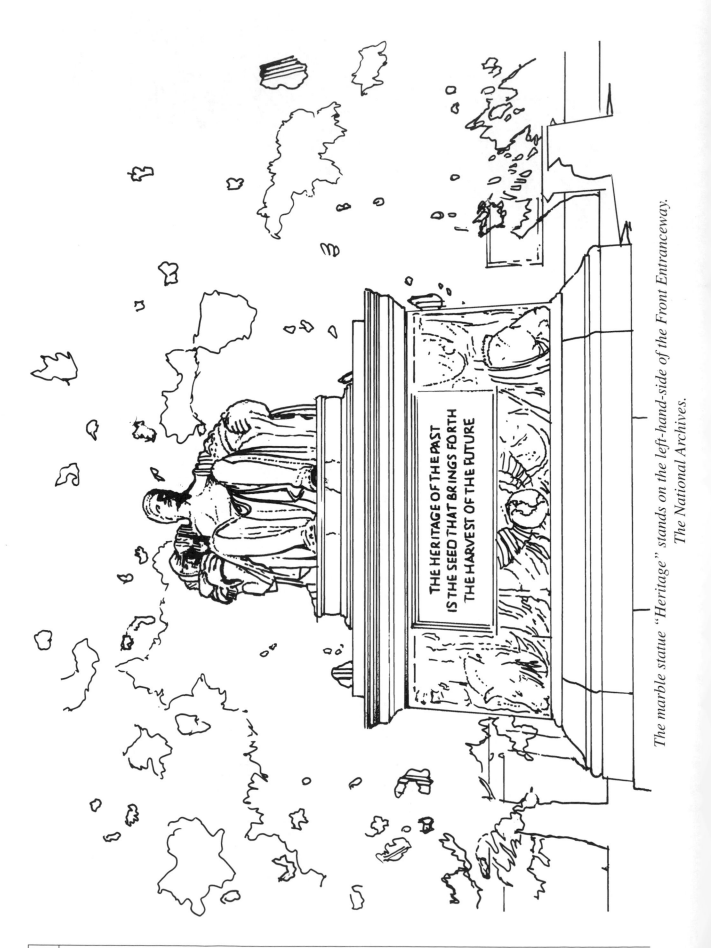

The marble statue "Heritage" stands on the left-hand-side of the Front Entranceway.
The National Archives.

The Christian Heritage Of Our Nation - History Curriculum

Seal of the National Archives of the United States.
The Ten Commandments (Exodus 20) stand out in predominance.

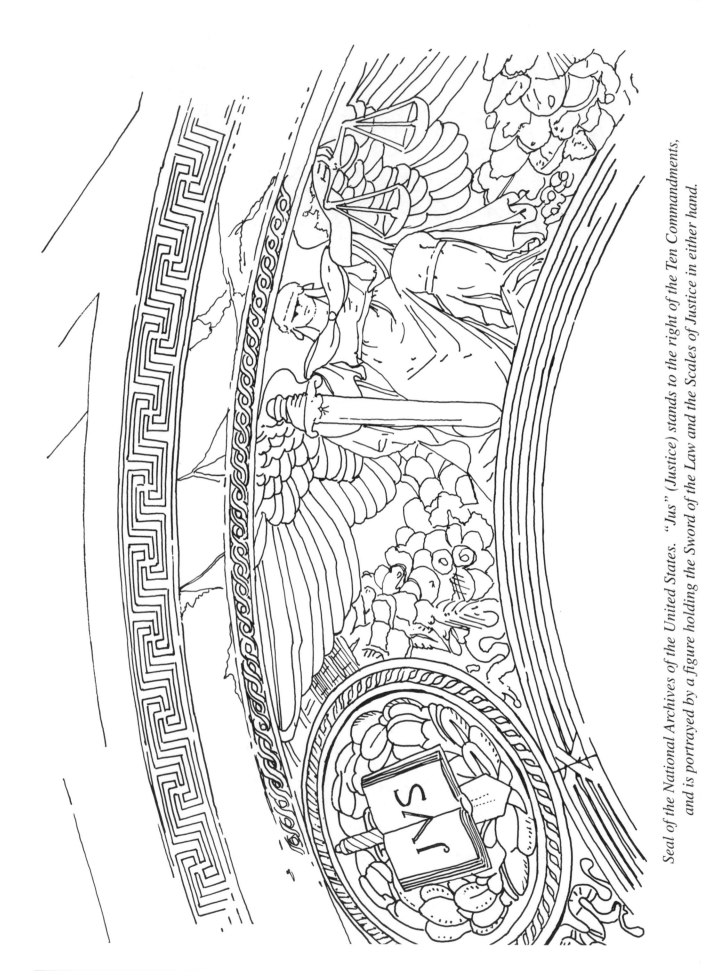

Seal of the National Archives of the United States. "Jus" (Justice) stands to the right of the Ten Commandments, and is portrayed by a figure holding the Sword of the Law and the Scales of Justice in either hand.

The Christian Heritage Of Our Nation - History Curriculum

LESSON 7

THE NATIONAL ARCHIVES

Unless the Lord builds the house, its builders labor in vain. Unless the Lord watches over the city, the watchmen stand guard in vain. — Psalm 127:1

The Declaration of Independence, the *U.S. Constitution*, and the *U.S. Bill of Rights* form the foundational documents of our nation. These original documents are housed within the National Archives, in our nation's capital. The two historical figures most closely associated with these writings are Thomas Jefferson, author of *The Declaration of Independence*; and George Washington, first President of the United States.

The following words of wisdom are inscribed on statues flanking each side of the Constitution Avenue entranceway to our National Archives:

"The Heritage of the Past is the Seed that brings forth the
Harvest of the Future"
and
"Eternal Vigilance is the Price of Liberty"

On the upper, central attic wall, facing Constitution Avenue, we glean the following message:

The ties that bind the lives of our people in one indissoluble union are perpetuated in the Archives of our government and to their custody this building is dedicated.

Upon the left-hand-side exterior attic walls, the purpose for which our National Archives came into being is clearly outlined in two-feet tall lettering:

The Glory and Romance of our History are here Preserved in the Chronicles of those who Conceived and Builded the Structure of our nation.

The right-hand exterior attic walls show forth its function:

This Building holds in trust the Records of our National Life and symbolizes our Faith in the Permanency of our National institutions.

Construction for the National Archives building, designed by architect John Russell Pope, began in 1932, and was completed in 1937. Handsome Corinthian columns encircle the structure. Two seated statues flanking its main entranceway represent *Heritage* and *Guardianship*. Both sculptures were the work of James Earle Fraser. The neoclassical female figure entitled *Heritage* symbolizes the role of the government in defending the sanctity of the home and family. The woman holds a child and a sheaf of wheat in her right hand, while the urn under her left hand symbolizes the Home. *Guardianship* is represented by a male personage holding in one hand the helmet of protection and in the other, a sheathed sword, together with *fasces*, the Roman symbol of Unified Government.

Two 38-foot, 7-inch tall bronze doors, each weighing 6.5 tons, slide into the walls, only to be seen before or at the close of a working day.

A large, circular, bronze design is embossed in the marble floor of the inner entranceway to the Rotunda. It represents the seal of the National Archives. The four allegorical, winged figures represent *Legislation, Justice, History,* and *War* and *Defense* — indicative of the documents housed within this structure. Interestingly enough, God's magnificent Ten Commandments stand out in prominence with the *Senate* and *Justice* to the right, symbolizing our legislative and judicial systems of government, and showing forth from whence America's power is derived.

Upon entering the Rotunda, one is greeted by two large murals on either side, entitled: *The Declaration of Independence*, and *The Constitution*. They were painted by New York's Barry Faulkner in the 1930's.

The Rotunda, or Great Hall, houses three items of great value preserved in the helium-filled bronze and glass display cases. These are the original, handwritten parchments upon which our republic is based: *The Declaration of Independence, The Constitution*, and *The Bill of Rights*.

The Declaration of Independence

The Declaration of Independence, forerunner to our *Constitution*, is founded upon the Word of God. Composed by Thomas Jefferson, it begins with an acknowledgment that man's freedom and equality was bestowed upon him by Almighty God.

> . . .We hold these truths to be self-evident, that all men are created equal, that they are endowed by their Creator with certain unalienable rights, that among these are life, liberty, and the pursuit of happiness. That to secure these rights, governments are instituted among men, deriving their just powers from the consent of the governed. That whenever any form of government becomes destructive of these ends, it is the right of the people to alter or to abolish it, and to institute new government, laying its foundation on such principles, and organizing its powers in such form as to them shall seem most likely to effect their safety and happiness. . .

A compilation of 27 grievances against the current power are then cited, after which a final conclusion is drawn:

> We, therefore, the Representatives of the United States of America, in General Congress assembled, appealing to the Supreme Judge of the world for the

The Christian Heritage Of Our Nation - History Curriculum

rectitude of our intentions, do, in the name, and by authority of the good people of these Colonies, solemnly publish and declare, That these United Colonies are, and of right ought to be, Free and Independent states;. . .And for the support of this declaration, with a firm reliance on the protection of Divine Providence, we mutually pledge to each other our lives, our fortunes, and our sacred honor.

Signed by order and in behalf of Congress,
John Hancock, President

The Constitution

In speaking about the *Constitution* of the United States, several U.S. presidents have traced its effectiveness and solidity to the hand of Almighty God. In his *Farewell Address* to the nation delivered in 1796, George Washington, our first president, spoke about its value in these terms:

May Heaven continue to you the choicest tokens of its beneficence: that your union and brotherly affection may be perpetual: that the free Constitution, which is the work of your hands, may be sacredly maintained; that its administration in every department may be stamped with wisdom and virtue; that, in fine, the happiness of the people of these states, under the auspices of liberty, may be made complete by so careful a preservation and so prudent a use of this blessing as will acquire them the glory of recommending it to the applause, the affection and adoption of every nation which is yet a stranger to it. . .It is of infinite moment that you should properly estimate the immense value of your national union to your collective and individual happiness;. . . The name American, which belongs to you in your national capacity, must always exult the just pride of patriotism more than any appellation derived from local discriminations.

William Henry Harrison, ninth U.S. president, stated:

It is union that we want, not of a party for the sake of that party, but a union of the whole country, for the sake of the whole country, for the defense of its interests and its honor against foreign aggression, for the defense of those principles for which our ancestors so gloriously contended.

John Tyler, our tenth president, stated:

Our prayers should evermore be offered up to the Father of the Universe for His wisdom to direct us in the path of our duty so as to enable us to consummate these high purposes.

Franklin Pierce, 14th president, boldly proclaimed:

It is with me an earnest and vital belief that as the Union has been the source, under Providence, of our prosperity to this time, so it is the surest pledge of a continuance of the blessing we have enjoyed, which we are sacredly bound to transmit undiminished to our children.

Andrew Johnson, 17th U.S. president, stood upon the conviction that:

> The hand of Divine Providence was never more plainly visible in the affairs of the men than in the framing and adopting of the Constitution.

Our 18th president, Gen. Ulysses S. Grant, prayed for the nation as follows:

> I ask patient forbearance one toward another throughout the land, and a determined effort on the part of every citizen to do his share toward cementing a happy union, and I ask the prayers of the nation to Almighty God in behalf of this consummation.

The 23rd president, Benjamin Harrison, concluded:

> God has placed upon our head a diadem and has laid at our feet power and wealth beyond definition or calculation. But we must not forget that we take these gifts upon the condition that justice and mercy shall hold the reins of power and that the upward avenues of hope shall be free to all people.

Theodore Roosevelt, 26th president, shed further light on the heritage which is now ours to enjoy:

> But we have faith that we shall not prove false to the memories of the men of the mighty past. They did their work, they left us the splendid heritage we now enjoy. We in our turn have an assured confidence that we shall be able to leave this heritage unwasted and enlarged to our children's children.

Reprinted below in their entirety are these three priceless documents of our unique Republic under God: *The Declaration of Independence*, the *U.S. Constitution*, and the *U.S. Bill of Rights,* along with Additional Amendments to the U.S. Constitution. Included therein is *The Virginia Declaration of Rights*, forerunner to the *U.S. Bill of Rights.*

THE DECLARATION OF INDEPENDENCE

WHEN IN THE COURSE OF HUMAN EVENTS it becomes necessary for one people to dissolve the political bands which have connected them with another, and to assume among the powers of the earth, the separate and equal station to which the Laws of Nature and Nature's God entitle them, a decent respect to the opinions of mankind requires that they should declare the causes which impel them to the separation.

We hold these truths to be self-evident, that all men are created equal, that they are endowed by their Creator with certain unalienable rights, that among these are life, liberty, and the pursuit of happiness. That to secure these rights, governments are instituted among men, deriving their just powers from the consent of the governed. That whenever any form of government becomes destructive of these ends, it is the right of the people to alter or to abolish it, and to institute new government, laying its foundation on such principles and organizing its powers in such form, as to them shall seem most likely to effect their safety and happiness. Prudence, indeed, will dictate that governments long established should not be changed for light and transient causes; and accordingly all experience hath shown, that mankind are more disposed to suffer, while evils are sufferable, than to right themselves by abolishing the forms to which they are accustomed. But when a long train of abuses and usurpations, pursuing invariably the same object, evinces a design to reduce them under absolute despotism, it is their right, it is their duty, to throw off such government, and to provide new guards for their future security. Such has been the patient sufferance of these Colonies; and such is now the necessity which constrains them to alter their former systems of government. The history of the present King of Great Britain is a history of repeated injuries and usurpations, all having, in direct object, the establishment of an absolute tyranny over these States. To prove this, let facts be submitted to a candid world.

He has refused his assent to laws, the most wholesome and necessary for the public good.

He has forbidden his Governors to pass laws of immediate and pressing importance, unless suspended in their operation till his assent should be obtained; and when so suspended, he has utterly neglected to attend to them.

He has refused to pass other laws for the accommodation of large districts of people, unless those people would relinquish the right of representation in the legislature, a right inestimable to them and formidable to tyrants only.

He has called together legislative bodies at places unusual, uncomfortable, and distant from the depository of their public records, for the sole purpose of fatiguing them into compliance with his measures.

He has dissolved representative houses repeatedly, for opposing with manly firmness his invasions on the rights of the people.

He has refused for a long time, after such dissolutions, to cause others to be elected; whereby the legislative powers, incapable of annihilation, have returned to the people at large for their exercise; the State remaining in the meantime exposed to all the dangers of invasion from without and convulsions within.

He has endeavoured to prevent the population of these states; for that purpose obstructing the laws of naturalization of foreigners; refusing to pass others to encourage their migration hither, and raising the conditions of new appropriations of lands.

He has obstructed the administration of justice, by refusing his assent to laws for establishing judiciary powers.

He has made judges dependent on his will alone, for the tenure of their offices, and the amount and payment of their salaries.

He has erected a multitude of new offices, and sent hither swarms of officers to harass our people, and eat out their substance.

He has kept among us, in times of peace, standing armies without the consent of our legislatures.

He has affected to render the military independent of, and superior to, the civil power.

He has combined with others to subject us to a jurisdiction foreign to our constitution, and unacknowledged by our laws; giving his assent to their acts of pretended legislation:

For quartering large bodies of armed troops among us:

For protecting them, by a mock trial, from punishment for any murders which they should commit on the inhabitants of these States:

For cutting off our trade with all parts of the world:

For imposing taxes on us without our consent:

For depriving us, in many cases, of the benefits of trial by jury:

For transporting us beyond seas to be tried for pretended offences:

For abolishing the free system of English laws in a neighbouring Province, establishing therein an arbitrary government, and enlarging its boundaries so as to render it at once an example and fit instrument for introducing the same absolute rule into these Colonies:

For taking away our Charters, abolishing our most valuable laws, and altering fundamentally the forms of our governments:

For suspending our own legislatures, and declaring themselves invested with power to legislate for us in all cases whatsoever.

He has abdicated government here, by declaring us out of his protection and waging war against us.

He has plundered our seas, ravaged our coasts, burnt our towns, and destroyed the lives of our people.

He is, at this time, transporting large armies of foreign mercenaries to complete the works of death, desolation and tyranny, already begun, with circumstances of cruelty and perfidy scarcely paralleled in the most barbarous ages, and totally unworthy the head of a civilized nation.

He has constrained our fellow citizens taken captive on the high seas to bear arms against their country, to become the executioners of their friends and brethren, or to fall themselves by their hands.

He has excited domestic insurrections amongst us, and has endeavoured to bring on the inhabitants of our frontiers, the merciless Indian savages, whose known rule of warfare is an undistinguished destruction of all ages, sexes, and conditions.

In every stage of these oppressions we have petitioned for redress in the most humble terms: our repeated petitions have been answered only by repeated injury. A prince whose character is thus marked by every act which may define a tyrant is unfit to be the ruler of a free people.

Nor have we been wanting in attention to our British brethren. We have warned them from time to time of attempts by their legislature to extend an unwarrantable jurisdiction over us. We have reminded them of the circumstances of our emigration and settlement here. We have appealed to their native justice and magnanimity, and we have conjured them by the ties of our common kindred to disavow these usurpations, which would inevitably interrupt our connections and correspondence. They too have been deaf to the voice of justice and consanguinity. We must, therefore, acquiesce in the necessity, which denounces our separation, and hold them, as we hold the rest of mankind, enemies in war, in peace, friends.

We, therefore, the Representatives of the United States of America, in General Congress assembled, appealing to the Supreme Judge of the world for the rectitude of our intentions, do, in the name, and by authority of the good people of these Colonies, solemnly publish and declare, That these United Colonies are, and of right ought to be, Free and Independent States; that they are absolved from all allegiance to the British Crown, and that all political connection between them and the State of Great Britain, is and ought to be totally dissolved; and that as Free and Independent States, they have full power to levy war, conclude peace, contract alliances, establish commerce, and to do all other acts and things which Independent States may of right do. And for the support of this declaration, with a firm reliance on the protection of Divine Providence, we mutually pledge to each other our lives, our fortunes, and our sacred honor.

John Hancock

NEW HAMPSHIRE
Josiah Bartlett
Wm. Whipple
Matthew Thornton

MASSACHUSETTS BAY
Saml. Adams
John Adams
Robt. Treat Paine
Elbridge Gerry

NEW YORK
Wm. Floyd
Phil. Livingston
Frans. Lewis
Lewis Morris

NORTH CAROLINA
Wm. Hooper
Joseph Hewes
John Penn

SOUTH CAROLINA
Edward Rutledge
Thos. Heyward, Junr.
Thomas Lynch, Junr.
Arthur Middleton

NEW JERSEY
Richd. Stockton
Jno. Witherspoon
Fras. Hopkinson
John Hart
Abra. Clark

RHODE ISLAND
Step. Hopkins
William Ellery

DELAWARE
Caesar Rodney
Geo. Read
Tho. M'Kean

MARYLAND
Samuel Chase
Wm. Paca
Thos. Stone
Charles Carroll of Carrollton

CONNECTICUT
Roger Sherman
Sam'el Huntington
Wm. Williams
Oliver Wolcott

GEORGIA
Button Gwinnett
Lyman Hall
Geo. Walton

PENNSYLVANIA
Robt. Morris
Benjamin Rush
Benja. Franklin
John Morton
Geo. Clymer
Jas. Smith
Geo. Taylor
James Wilson
Geo. Ross

VIRGINIA
George Wythe
Richard Henry Lee
Th. Jefferson
Benja. Harrison
Ths. Nelson, Jr.
Francis Lightfoot Lee
Carter Braxton

July 4th, 1776

THE U.S. CONSTITUTION

WE, THE PEOPLE of the United States, in order to form a more perfect union, establish justice, insure domestic tranquility, provide for the common defense, promote the general welfare, and secure the Blessings of Liberty to ourselves and our posterity, do ordain and establish this Constitution for the United States of America.

ARTICLE I

Section 1. All legislative powers herein granted shall be vested in a Congress of the United States, which shall consist of a Senate and House of Representatives.

Section 2. 1. The House of Representatives shall be composed of members chosen every second year by the people of the several States, and the electors in each State shall have the qualifications requisite for electors of the most numerous branch of the State legislature.

2. No person shall be a representative who shall not have attained to the age of twenty-five years, and been seven years a citizen of the United States, and who shall not, when elected, be an inhabitant of that State in which he shall be chosen.

3. Representatives and direct taxes shall be apportioned among the several States which may be included within this Union, according to their respective numbers, which shall be determined by adding to the whole number of free persons, including those bound to service for a term of years, and excluding Indians not taxed, *three fifths of all other persons.* The actual enumeration shall be made within three years after the first meeting of the Congress of the United States, and within every subsequent term of ten years, in such manner as they shall by law direct. The number of representatives shall not exceed one for every thirty thousand, but each State shall have at least one representative; and until such enumeration shall be made, the State of New Hampshire shall be entitled to choose three, Massachusetts eight, Rhode Island and Providence Plantations one, Connecticut five, New York six, New Jersey four, Pennsylvania eight, Delaware one, Maryland six, Virginia ten, North Carolina five, South Carolina five, and Georgia three.

4. When vacancies happen in the representation from any State, the executive authority thereof shall issue writs of election to fill such vacancies.

5. The House of Representatives shall choose their speaker and other officers; and shall have the sole power of impeachment.

Section 3. 1. The Senate of the United States shall be composed of two senators from each State, *chosen by the legislature thereof,* for six years; and each senator shall have one vote.

2. Immediately after they shall be assembled in consequence of the first election, they shall be divided as equally as may be into three classes. The seats of the senators of the first class shall be vacated at the expiration of the second year, of the second class at the expiration of the fourth year, and of the third class at the expiration of the sixth year, so that one third may be chosen every second year; and if vacancies happen by resignation, or otherwise, during the recess of the legislature of any State, the executive thereof may make temporary appointments until the next meeting of the legislature, which shall then fill such vacancies.

3. No person shall be a senator who shall not have attained to the age of thirty years, and been nine years a citizen of the United States, and who shall not, when elected, be an inhabitant of that State for which he shall be chosen.

4. The Vice-President of the United States shall be President of the Senate, but shall have no vote, unless they be equally divided.

5. The Senate shall choose their other officers, and also a president *pro tempore*, in the absence of the Vice-President, or when he shall exercise the office of the President of the United States.

6. The Senate shall have the sole power to try all impeachments. When sitting for that purpose, they shall be on oath or affirmation. When the President of the United States is tried, the chief justice shall preside: and no person shall be convicted without the concurrence of two thirds of the members present.

7. Judgment in cases of impeachment shall not extend further than to removal from office, and disqualifications to hold and enjoy any office of honor, trust or profit under the United States: but the party convicted shall nevertheless be liable and subject to indictment, trial, judgment and punishment, according to law.

Section 4. 1. The times, places, and manner of holding elections for senators and representatives, shall be prescribed in each state by the legislature thereof; but the Congress may at any time by law make or alter such regulations, except as to the places of choosing senators.

2. The Congress shall assemble at least once in every year, and such meeting shall be on the first Monday in December, unless they shall by law appoint a different day.

Section 5. 1. Each House shall be the judge of the elections, returns and qualifications of its own members, and a majority of each shall constitute a quorum to do business; but a smaller number may adjourn from day to day, and may be authorized to compel the attendance of absent members, in such manner, and under such penalties as each House may provide.

2. Each House may determine the rules of its proceedings, punish its members for disorderly behavior, and, with the concurrence of two thirds, expel a member.

The Christian Heritage Of Our Nation - History Curriculum

3. Each House shall keep a journal of its proceedings, and from time to time publish the same, excepting such parts as may in their judgment require secrecy; and the yeas and nays of the members of either House on any question shall, at the desire of one fifth of those present, be entered on the journal.

4. Neither House, during the session of Congress, shall, without the consent of the other, adjourn for more than three days, nor to any other place than that in which the two Houses shall be sitting.

Section 6. 1. The senators and representatives shall receive a compensation for their services, to be ascertained by law, and paid out of the Treasury of the United States. They shall in all cases, except treason, felony, and breach of the peace, be privileged from arrest during their attendance at the session of their respective Houses, and in going to and returning from the same; and for any speech or debate in either House, they shall not be questioned in any other place.

2. No senator or representative shall, during the time for which he was elected, be appointed to any civil office under the authority of the United States, which shall have been created, or the emoluments whereof shall have been increased during such time; and no person holding any office under the United States shall be a member of either House during his continuance in office.

Section 7. 1. All bills for raising revenue shall originate in the House of Representatives; but the Senate may propose or concur with amendments as on other bills.

2. Every bill which shall have passed the House of Representatives and the Senate, shall, before it becomes a law, be presented to the President of the United States; if he approve he shall sign it, but if not he shall return it, with his objections, to that House in which it shall have originated, who shall enter the objections at large on their journal, and proceed to reconsider it. If after such reconsideration two thirds of that House shall agree to pass the bill, it shall be sent, together with the objections, to the other House, by which it shall likewise be reconsidered, and if approved by two thirds of that House, it shall become a law. But in all such cases the votes of both Houses shall be determined by yeas and nays, and the names of the persons voting for and against the bill shall be entered on the journal of each House respectively. If any bill shall not be returned by the President within ten days (Sundays excepted) after it shall have been presented to him, the same shall be a law, in like manner as if he had signed it, unless the Congress by their adjournment prevent its return, in which case it shall not be a law.

3. Every order, resolution, or vote to which the concurrence of the Senate and the House of Representatives may be necessary (except on a question of adjournment) shall be presented to the President of the United States; and before the same shall take effect, shall be approved by him, or being disapproved by him, shall be repassed by two thirds of the Senate and House of Representatives, according to the rules and

limitations prescribed in the case of a bill.

Section 8. The Congress shall have the power

1. To lay and collect taxes, duties, imposts, and excises, to pay the debts and provide for the common defense and general welfare of the United States; but all duties, imposts, and excises shall be uniform throughout the United States;

2. To borrow money on the credit of the United States;

3. To regulate commerce with foreign nations, and among the several States, and with the Indian tribes;

4. To establish a uniform rule of naturalization, and uniform laws on the subject of bankruptcies throughout the United States;

5. To coin money, regulate the value thereof, and of foreign coin, and fix the standard of weights and measures.

6. To provide for the punishment of counterfeiting the securities and current coin of the United States;

7. To establish post offices and post roads;

8. To promote the progress of science and useful arts, by securing for limited times to authors and inventors the exclusive right to their respective writings and discoveries;

9. To constitute tribunals inferior to the Supreme Court;

10. To define and punish piracies and felonies committed on the high seas, and offenses against the law of nations;

11. To declare war, grant letters of marque and reprisal, and make rules concerning captures on land and water;

12. To raise and support armies, but no appropriation of money to that use shall be for a longer term than two years;

13. To provide and maintain a navy;

14. To make rules for the government and regulation of the land and naval forces;

15. To provide for calling forth the militia to execute the laws of the Union, suppress insurrections and repel invasions;

16. To provide for organizing, arming, and disciplining the militia, and for governing such part of them as may be employed in the service of the United States, reserving to

the States respectively, the appointment of the officers, and the authority of training the militia according to the discipline prescribed by Congress;

17. To exercise exclusive legislation in all cases whatsoever, over such district (not exceeding ten miles square) as may, by cession of particular States, and the acceptance of Congress, become the seat of the government of the United States, and to exercise like authority over all places purchased by the consent of the legislature of the State in which the same shall be, for the erection of forts, magazines, arsenals, dockyards, and other needful buildings; and

18. To make all laws which shall be necessary and proper for carrying into execution the foregoing powers, and all other powers vested by this Constitution in the government of the United States, or in any department or officer thereof.

Section 9. 1. The migration or importation of such persons as any of the States now existing shall think proper to admit, shall not be prohibited by the Congress prior to the year one thousand eight hundred and eight, but a tax or duty may be imposed on such importation, not exceeding ten dollars for each person.

2. The privilege of the writ of *habeas corpus* shall not be suspended, unless when in cases of rebellion or invasion the public safety may require it.

3. No bill of attainder or *ex post facto* law shall be passed.

4. No capitation, or other direct, tax shall be laid, unless in proportion to the census or enumeration hereinbefore directed to be taken.

5. No tax or duty shall be laid on articles exported from any State.

6. No preference shall be given by any regulation of commerce or revenue to the ports of one State over those of another: nor shall vessels bound to, or from, one State be obliged to enter, clear, or pay duties in another.

7. No money shall be drawn from the treasury, but in consequence of appropriations made by law; and a regular statement and account of the receipts and expenditures of all public money shall be published from time to time.

8. No title of nobility shall be granted by the United States: and no person holding any office of profit or trust under them, shall, without the consent of the Congress, accept of any present, emolument, office, or title, of any kind whatever, from any king, prince, or foreign State.

Section 10. 1. No State shall enter into any treaty, alliance, or confederation; grant letters of marque and reprisal; coin money; emit bills of credit, make anything but gold and silver coin a tender in payment of debts; pass any bill of attainder, *ex post facto* law, or law impairing the obligation of contracts, or grant any title of nobility.

2. No State shall, without the consent of the Congress, lay any imposts or duties on imports or exports, except what may be absolutely necessary for executing its inspection laws; and the net produce of all duties and imposts laid by any State on imports or exports, shall be for the use of the Treasury of the United States; and all such laws shall be subject to the revision and control of the Congress.

3. No State shall, without the consent of the Congress, lay any duty of tonnage, keep troops, or ships of war in time of peace, enter into any agreement or compact with another State, or with a foreign power, or engage in war, unless actually invaded, or in such imminent danger as will not admit of delay.

ARTICLE II

Section 1. 1. The executive power shall be vested in a President of the United States of America. He shall hold his office during the term of four years, and, together with the Vice President, chosen for the same term, be elected as follows:

2. Each State shall appoint, in such manner as the legislature thereof may direct, a number of electors, equal to the whole number of senators and representatives to which the State may be entitled in the Congress: but no senator or representative, or person holding an office of trust or profit under the United States, shall be appointed an elector.

The electors shall meet in their respective States, and vote by ballot for two persons, of whom one at least shall not be an inhabitant of the same State with themselves. And they shall make a list of all the persons voted for, and of the number of votes for each; which list they shall sign and certify, and transmit sealed to the seat of the government of the United States, directed to the President of the Senate. The President of the Senate shall, in the presence of the Senate and House of Representatives, open all the certificates, and the votes shall then be counted. The person having the greatest number of votes shall be the President, if such number be a majority of the whole number of electors appointed; and if there be more than one who have such majority, and have an equal number of votes, then the House of Representatives shall immediately choose by ballot one of them for President; and if no person have a majority, then from the five highest on the list the said House shall in like manner choose the President. But in choosing the President, the votes shall be taken by States, the representation from each State having one vote; a quorum for this purpose shall consist of a member or members from two thirds of the States, and a majority of all the States shall be necessary to a choice. In every case, after the choice of the President, the person having the greatest number of votes of the electors shall be the Vice President. But if there should remain two or more who have equal votes, the Senate shall choose from them by ballot the Vice President.

3. The Congress may determine the time of choosing the electors, and the day on which they shall give their votes; which day shall be the same throughout the United States.

4. No person except a natural born citizen, or a citizen of the United States at the time of the adoption of this Constitution, shall be eligible to the office of President; neither shall any person be eligible to that office who shall not have attained to the age of thirty-five years, and been fourteen years a resident within the United States.

5. In case of the removal of the President from office, or of his death, resignation, or inability to discharge the powers and duties of the said office, the same shall devolve on the Vice President, and the Congress may by law provide for the case of removal, death, resignation, or inability, both of the President and Vice President, declaring what officer shall then act as President, and such officer shall act accordingly, until the disability be removed, or a President shall be elected.

6. The President shall, at stated times, receive for his services a compensation, which shall neither be increased nor diminished during the period for which he shall have been elected, and he shall not receive within that period any other emolument from the United States, or any of them.

7. Before he enter on the execution of his office, he shall take the following oath or affirmation:— "I do solemnly swear (or affirm) that I will faithfully execute the office of President of the United States, and will to the best of my ability, preserve, protect and defend the Constitution of the United States."

Section 2. 1. The President shall be Commander-in-chief of the Army and Navy of the United States, and of the militia of the several States, when called into the actual service of the United States; he may require the opinion, in writing, of the principal officer in each of the executive departments, upon any subject relating to the duties of their respective offices, and he shall have power to grant reprieves and pardons for offenses against the United States, except in cases of impeachment.

2. He shall have power, by and with the advice and consent of the Senate, to make treaties, provided two-thirds of the senators present concur; and he shall nominate, and by and with the advice and consent of the Senate, shall appoint ambassadors, other public ministers and consuls, judges of the Supreme Court, and all other officers of the United States, whose appointments are not herein otherwise provided for, and which shall be established by law: but the Congress may by law vest the appointment of such inferior officers, as they think proper, in the President alone, in the courts of law, or in the heads of departments.

3. The President shall have power to fill up all vacancies that may happen during the recess of the Senate, by granting commissions which shall expire at the end of their next session.

Section 3. He shall from time to time give to the Congress information of the state of the Union, and recommend to their consideration such measures as he shall judge necessary and expedient; he may, on extraordinary occasions, convene both Houses, or either of them, and in case of disagreement between them with respect to the time of adjournment, he may adjourn them to such time as he shall think proper; he shall receive ambassadors and other public ministers; he shall take care that the laws be faithfully executed, and shall commission all the officers of the United States.

Section 4. The President, Vice President, and all civil officers of the United States, shall be removed from office on impeachment for, and conviction of, treason, bribery, or other high crimes and misdemeanors.

ARTICLE III

Section 1. The judicial power of the United States shall be vested in one Supreme Court, and in such inferior courts as the Congress may from time to time ordain and establish. The judges, both of the Supreme and inferior courts, shall hold their offices during good behavior, and shall, at stated times, receive for their services, a compensation which shall not be diminished during their continuance in office.

Section 2. 1. The judicial power shall extend to all cases, in law and equity, arising under this Constitution, the laws of the United States, and treaties made, or which shall be made, under their authority;—to all cases affecting ambassadors, other public ministers and consuls;—to all cases of admiralty and maritime jurisdiction;—to controversies to which the United States shall be a party;—to controversies between two or more States;—between a State and citizens of another State;—between citizens of different States;—between citizens of the same State claiming lands under grants of different States, and between a State, or the citizens thereof, and foreign States, citizens or subjects.

2. In all cases affecting ambassadors, other public ministers and consuls, and those in which a State shall be party, the Supreme Court shall have original jurisdiction. In all the other cases before mentioned, the Supreme Court shall have appellate jurisdiction, both as to law and to fact, with such exceptions, and under such regulations as the Congress shall make.

3. The trial of all crimes, except in cases of impeachment, shall be by jury; and such trial shall be held in the State where the said crimes shall have been committed; but when not committed within any State, the trial shall be at such place or places as the Congress may by law have directed.

Section 3. 1. Treason against the United States shall consist only in levying war against them, or in adhering to their enemies, giving them aid and comfort. No person shall be convicted of treason unless on the testimony of two witnesses to the same overt act, or on confession in open court.

2. The Congress shall have power to declare the punishment of treason, but no attainder of treason shall work corruption of blood, or forfeiture except during the life of the person attained.

ARTICLE IV

Section 1. Full faith and credit shall be given in each State to the public acts, records, and judicial proceedings of every other State. And the Congress may by general laws prescribe the manner in which such acts, records and proceedings shall be proved, and the effect thereof.

Section 2. 1. The citizens of each State shall be entitled to all privileges and immunities of citizens in the several States.

2. A person charged in any State with treason, felony, or other crime, who shall flee from justice, and be found in another State, shall, on demand of the executive authority of the State from which he fled, be delivered up to be removed to the State having jurisdiction of the crime.

3. No person held to service or labor in one State under the laws thereof, escaping into another, shall, in consequence of any law or regulation therein, be discharged from such service or labor, but shall be delivered up on claim of the party to whom such service or labor may be due.

Section 3. 1. New States may be admitted by the Congress into this Union; but no new State shall be formed or erected within the jurisdiction of any other State; nor any State be formed by the junction of two or more States, or parts of States, without the consent of the legislatures of the States concerned as well as of the Congress.

2. The Congress shall have power to dispose of and make all needful rules and regulations respecting the territory or other property belonging to the United States; and nothing in this Constitution shall be so construed as to prejudice any claims of the United States, or of any particular State.

Section 4. The United States shall guarantee to every State in this Union a republican form of government, and shall protect each of them against invasion; and on application of the legislature, or of the executive (when the legislature cannot be convened), against domestic violence.

ARTICLE V

The Congress, whenever two thirds of both Houses shall deem it necessary, shall propose amendments to this Constitution, or, on the application of the legislatures of two-thirds of the several States, shall call a convention for proposing amendments, which, in either case, shall be valid to all intents and purposes, as part of this Constitution, when ratified by the legislatures of three-fourths of the several States, or by conventions in three-fourths thereof, as the one or the other mode of ratification may be proposed by the Congress; Provided that no amendment which may be made prior to the year one thousand eight hundred and eight shall in any manner affect the first and fourth clauses in the ninth section of the first article; and that no State, without its consent, shall be deprived of its equal suffrage in the Senate.

ARTICLE VI

1. All debts contracted and engagements entered into, before the adoption of this Constitution, shall be as valid against the United States under this Constitution, as under the Confederation.

2. This Constitution, and the laws of the United States which shall be made in pursuance thereof, and all treaties made, or which shall be made, under the authority of the United States, shall be the supreme law of the land; and the Judges in every State shall be bound thereby, anything in the Constitution or laws of any State to the contrary notwithstanding.

3. The senators and representatives before mentioned, and the members of the several State legislatures, and all executive and judicial officers, both of the United States and of the several States, shall be bound by oath or affirmation to support this Constitution; but no religious test shall ever be required as a qualification to any office or public trust under the United States.

ARTICLE VII

The ratification of the conventions of nine States shall be sufficient for the establishment of this Constitution between the States so ratifying the same.

> Done in Convention by the unanimous consent of the States present the seventeenth day of September in the year of our Lord [Jesus Christ]* one thousand seven hundred and eighty-seven, and of the independence of the United States of America the twelfth. In witness whereof we have hereunto subscribed our names.
>
> *George Washington*, President, and Deputy from Virginia

*Editor's parentheses

NEW HAMPSHIRE
John Langdon
Nicholas Gilman

MASSACHUSETTS
Nathaniel Gorham
Rufus King

CONNECTICUT
William Samuel Johnson
Roger Sherman

NEW YORK
Alexander Hamilton

NEW JERSEY
William Livinston
David Brearley
William Paterson
Jonathan Dayton

PENNSYLVANIA
Benjamin Franklin
Thomas Mifflin
Robert Morris
George Clymer
Thomas Fitzsimons
Jared Ingersoll
James Wilson
Gouverneur Morris

DELAWARE
George Read
Gunning Bedford, Junior
John Dickinson
Richard Bassett
Jacob Broom

MARYLAND
James McHenry
Daniel of St. Tho. Jenifer
Daniel Carrol

VIRGINIA
John Blair
James Madison, Junior

NORTH CAROLINA
William Blount
Richard Dobbs Spaight
Hugh Williamson

SOUTH CAROLINA
John Rutledge
Charles Cotesworth Pinckney
Charles Pinckney
Pierce Butler

GEORGIA
William Few
Abraham Baldwin

Attest, William Jackson, Secretary

THE VIRGINIA DECLARATION OF RIGHTS

The Virginia Declaration of Rights, authored by founding father George Mason, is the forerunner to the U.S. Bill of Rights. It is a unique, American Christian document, commencing as follows:

A Declaration of Rights made by the Representatives of the good people of Virginia, assembled in full and free Convention; which rights do pertain to them and their posterity, as the basis and foundation of government.

ARTICLE I

THAT all men are by nature equally free and independent, and have certain inherent rights, of which, when they enter into a state of society, they cannot, by any compact, deprive or divest their posterity; namely, the enjoyment of life and liberty, with the means of acquiring and possessing property, and pursuing and obtaining happiness and safety.

ARTICLE II

THAT all power is vested in, and consequently derived from, the people; that magistrates are their trustees and servants, and at all times amendable to them.

ARTICLE III

THAT government is, or ought to be, instituted for the common benefit, protection, and security, of the people, nation, or community; of all the various modes and forms of government that is best, which is capable of producing the greatest degree of happiness and safety, and is most effectually secured against the danger of mal-administration; and that, whenever any government shall be found inadequate or contrary to these purposes, a majority of the community hath an indubitable, unalienable, and indefeasible right, to reform, alter, or abolish it, in such manner as shall be judged most conducive to the public weal.

ARTICLE IV

THAT no man, or set of men, are entitled to exclusive or separate emoluments or privileges from the community, but in consideration of public service; which, not being descendible, neither ought the offices of Magistrate, Legislator, or Judge, to be hereditary.

ARTICLE V

THAT the legislative and executive powers of the state should be separate and distinct from the judicative; and, that the members of the two first may be restrained from oppression, by feeling and participating in the burthens of the people, they should, at fixed periods, be reduced to a private station, return into that body from which they were originally taken, and the vacancies be supplied by frequent, certain, and regular elections, in which all, or any part of the former members, to be again eligible, or ineligible, as the laws shall direct.

ARTICLE VI

THAT elections of members to serve as Representatives of the people, in assembly, ought to be free; and that all men, having sufficient evidence of permanent common interest with the attachment to the community, have the right of suffrage, and cannot be taxed or deprived of their property for public uses without their own consent or that of their representatives so elected, nor bound by any law to which they have not, in like manner, assented for the public good.

ARTICLE VII

THAT all power of suspending laws, or the execution of laws, by any authority without consent of the Representatives of the people, is injurious to their rights, and ought not to be exercised.

ARTICLE VIII

THAT in all capital or criminal prosecutions a man hath a right to demand the cause and nature of his accusation, to be confronted with the accusers and witnesses, to call for evidence in his favour, and to a speedy trial by an impartial jury of his vicinage without whose unanimous consent he cannot be found guilty, nor can he be compelled to give evidence against himself; that no man be deprived of his liberty except by the law of the land, or the judgement of his peers.

ARTICLE IX

THAT excessive bail ought not to be required, nor excessive fines imposed; nor cruel and unusual punishments inflicted.

ARTICLE X

THAT general warrants, whereby any officer or messenger may be commanded to search suspected places without evidence of a fact committed, or to seize any person or persons not named, or whose offence is not particularly described and supported by evidence, are grievous and oppressive, and ought not to be granted.

ARTICLE XI

THAT in controversies respecting property, and in suits between man and man, the ancient trail by jury is preferable to any other, and ought to be held sacred.

ARTICLE XII

THAT the freedom of the press is one of the greatest bulwarks of liberty, and can never be restrained but by despotic governments.

ARTICLE XIII

THAT a well regulated militia, composed of the body of the people, trained to arms, is the proper, natural, and safe defense of a free state; that standing armies, in time of peace, should be avoided, as dangerous to liberty; and that, in all cases, that the military should be under strict subordination to, and governed by, the Civil Power.

ARTICLE XIV

THAT the people have a right to uniform government; and therefore, that no Government; separate from, the Government of Virginia, ought to be erected or established within the limits thereof.

ARTICLE XV

THAT no free Government, or the blessing of liberty, can be preserved to any people but by a firm adherence to justice, moderation, temperance, frugality, and virtue, and by frequent recurrence to fundamental principles.

ARTICLE XVI

THAT Religion, or the duty which we owe to our Creator, and manner of discharging it, can be directed only by reason and conviction, not by force or violence; and therefore, all men are equally entitled to the free exercise of Religion, according to the dictates of conscience; and that it is the mutal duty of all to practice Christian forbearance, love and charity, towards each other.

Drawn originally by George Mason and adopted unanimously by the Convention of Delegates at the Capitol in Williamsburg on June 12, 1776.

THE BILL OF RIGHTS
FIRST TEN AMENDMENTS TO THE U.S. CONSTITUTION

ARTICLE I

Congress shall make no law respecting an establishment of religion, or prohibiting the free exercise thereof; or abridging the freedom of speech, or of the press; or the right of the people peaceably to assemble, and to petition the government for a redress of grievances.

ARTICLE II

A well regulated militia being necessary to the security of a free State, the right of the people to keep and bear arms shall not be infringed.

ARTICLE III

No soldier shall, in time of peace, be quartered in any house, without the consent of the owner, nor in time of war, but in a manner to be prescribed by law.

ARTICLE IV

The right of the people to be secure in their persons, houses, papers, and effects, against unreasonable searches and seizures, shall not be violated, and no warrants shall issue, but upon probable cause, supported by oath or affirmation, and particularly describing the place to be searched, and the persons or things to be seized.

ARTICLE V

No person shall be held to answer for a capital, or otherwise infamous crime, unless on a presentment or indictment of a grand jury, except in cases arising in the land or naval forces, or in the militia, when in actual service in time of war or public danger; nor shall any person be subject for the same offense to be twice put in jeopardy of life or limb; nor shall be compelled in any criminal case to be a witness against himself, nor be deprived of life, liberty, or property, without due process of law; nor shall private property be taken for public use without just compensation.

ARTICLE VI

In all criminal prosecutions, the accused shall enjoy the right to a speedy and public trial, by an impartial jury of the State and district wherein the crime shall have been committed, which district shall have been previously ascertained by law, and to be informed of the nature and cause of the accusation; to be confronted with the witnesses against him; to have compulsory process for obtaining witnesses in his favor, and to have the assistance of counsel for his defense.

ARTICLE VII

In suits at common law, where the value in controversy shall exceed twenty dollars, the right of trial by jury shall be preserved, and no fact tried by a jury shall be otherwise reexamined in any court of the United States, than according to the rules of the common law.

ARTICLE VIII

Excessive bail shall not be required, nor excessive fines imposed, nor cruel and unusual punishments inflicted.

ARTICLE IX

The enumeration in the Constitution of certain rights shall not be construed to deny or disparage others retained by the people.

ARTICLE X

The powers not delegated to the United States by the Constitution, nor prohibited by it to the States, are reserved to the States respectively, or to the people.

The Christian Heritage Of Our Nation - History Curriculum

ARTICLE XI

Passed by Congress March 5, 1794   Ratified January 8, 1798

The judicial power of the United States shall not be construed to extend to any suit in law or equity, commenced or prosecuted against one of the United States by citizens of another State, or by citizens or subjects of any foreign State.

ARTICLE XII

Passed by Congress December 12, 1803   Ratified September 25, 1804

The electors shall meet in their respective States, and vote by ballot for President and Vice President, one of whom, at least, shall not be an inhabitant of the same State with themselves; they shall name in their ballots the person voted for as President, and in distinct ballots, the person voted for as Vice President, and they shall make distinct lists of all persons voted for as President and of all persons voted for as Vice President, and of the number of votes for each, which lists they shall sign and certify, and transmit sealed to the seat of the government of the United States, directed to the President of the Senate;—The President of the Senate shall, in the presence of the Senate and House of Representatives, open all the certificates and the votes shall then be counted;—The person having the greatest number of votes for President, shall be the President, if such number be a majority of the whole number of electors appointed; and if no person have such majority, then from the persons having the highest numbers not exceeding three on the list of those voted for as President, the House of Representatives shall choose immediately, by ballot, the President. But in choosing the President, the votes shall be taken by States, the representation from each State having one vote; a quorum for this purpose shall consist of a member or members from two-thirds of the States, and a majority of all the States shall be necessary to a choice. And if the House of Representatives shall not choose a President whenever the right of choice shall devolve upon them, before the fourth day of March next following, then the Vice President shall act as President, as in the case of the death or other constitutional disability of the President. The person having the greatest number of votes as Vice President shall be the Vice President, if such number be a majority of the whole number of electors appointed, and if no person have a majority, then from the two highest numbers on the list, the Senate shall choose the Vice President; a quorum for the purpose shall consist of two thirds of the whole number of Senators, and a majority of the whole number shall be necessary to a choice. But no person constitutionally ineligible to the office of President shall be eligible to that of Vice President of the United States.

ARTICLE XIII

Passed by Congress February 1, 1865   Ratified December 18, 1866

Section 1. Neither slavery nor involuntary servitude, except as punishment for crime whereof the party shall have been duly convicted, shall exist within the United States, or any place subject to their jurisdiction.

Section 2. Congress shall have power to enforce this article by appropriate legislation.

ARTICLE XIV

Passed by Congress June 16, 1866   Ratified July 28, 1868

Section 1. All persons born or naturalized in the United States, and subject to the jurisdiction thereof, are citizens of the United States and of the State wherein they reside. No State shall make or enforce any law which shall abridge the privileges or immunities of citizens of the United States; nor shall any State deprive any person of life, liberty, or property, without due process of law; nor deny to any person within its jurisdiction the equal protection of the laws.

Section 2. Representatives shall be apportioned among the several States according to their respective numbers, counting the whole number of persons in each State, excluding Indians not taxed. But when the right to vote at any election for the choice of electors for President and Vice President of the United States, representatives in Congress, the executive and judicial officers of a State, or the members of the legislature thereof, is denied to any of the male inhabitants of such State, being twenty-one years of age, and citizens of the United States, or in any way abridged, except for participation in rebellion, or other crime, the basis of representation therein shall be reduced in the proportion which the number of such male citizens shall bear to the whole number of male citizens twenty-one years of age in such State.

Section 3. No person shall be a senator or representative in Congress, or elector of President and Vice President, or hold any office, civil or military, under the United States, or under any State, who having previously taken an oath, as a member of Congress, or as an officer of the United States, or a member of any State legislature, or as an executive or judicial officer of any State, to support the Constitution of the United States, shall have engaged in insurrection or rebellion against the same, or given aid or comfort to the enemies thereof. But Congress may by a vote of two-thirds of each House, remove such disability.

Section 4. The validity of the public debt of the United States, authorized by law, including debts incurred for payment of pensions and bounties for services in suppressing insurrection or rebellion, shall not be questioned. But neither the United States nor any State shall assume or pay any debt or obligation incurred in aid of insurrection or rebellion against the United States, or any claim for the loss or emancipation of any slave; but all such debts, obligations, and claims shall be held illegal and void.

Section 5. The Congress shall have power to enforce, by appropriate legislation, the provisions of this article.

ARTICLE XV

Passed by Congress February 26, 1869   Ratified March 30, 1870

Section 1. The right of citizens of the United States to vote shall not be denied or abridged by the United States or by any State on account of race, color, or previous condition of servitude.

Section 2. The Congress shall have power to enforce this article by appropriate legislation.

ARTICLE XVI

Passed by Congress July 12, 1909   Ratified February 25, 1913

The Congress shall have power to lay and collect taxes on incomes, from whatever source derived, without apportionment among the several States, and without regard to any census or enumeration.

ARTICLE XVII

Passed by Congress May 16, 1912   Ratified May 31, 1913

Section 1. The Senate of the United States shall be composed of two senators from each State, elected by the people thereof, for six years; and each senator shall have one vote. The electors in each State shall have the qualifications requisite for electors of the most numerous branch of the State legislature.

Section 2. When vacancies happen in the representation of any State in the Senate, the executive authority of such State shall issue writs of election to fill such vacancies: *Provided,* That the legislature of any State may empower the executive thereof to make temporary appointments until the people fill the vacancies by election as the legislature may direct.

Section 3. This amendment shall not be so construed as to affect the election or term of any senator chosen before it becomes valid as part of the Constitution.

ARTICLE XVIII

Passed by Congress December 18, 1917   Ratified January 29, 1919

Section 1. After one year from the ratification of this article, the manufacture, sale, or transportation of intoxicating liquors within, the importation thereof into, or the exportation thereof from the United States and all territory subject to the jurisdiction thereof for beverage purposes is hereby prohibited.

Section 2. The Congress and the several States shall have concurrent power to enforce this article by appropriate legislation.

Section 3. This article shall be inoperative unless it shall have been ratified as an amendment to the Constitution by the legislatures of the several States, as provided in the Constitution, within seven years from the date of the submission hereof to the States by Congress.

ARTICLE XIX

Passed by Congress June 5, 1919   Ratified August 26, 1920

Section 1. The right of citizens of the United States to vote shall not be denied or abridged by the United States or by any State on account of sex.

Section 2. The Congress shall have power by appropriate legislation to enforce the provisions of this article.

ARTICLE XX

Passed by Congress March 3, 1932   Ratified February 6, 1933

Section 1. The terms of the President and Vice President shall end at noon on the 20th day of January, and the terms of Senators and Representatives at noon on the 3d day of January, of the years in which such terms would have ended if this article had not been ratified; and the terms of their successors shall then begin.

Section 2. The Congress shall assemble at least once in every year, and such meeting shall begin at noon on the 3d day of January, unless they shall by law appoint a different day.

Section 3. If, at the time fixed for the beginning of the term of the President, the President-elect shall have died, the Vice President-elect shall become President. If a President shall not have been chosen before the time fixed for the beginning of his term, or if the President-elect shall have failed to qualify, then the Vice President-elect shall act as President until a President shall have qualified; and the Congress may by law provide for the case wherein neither a President-elect nor a Vice President-elect shall have qualified, declaring who shall then act as President, or the manner in which one who is to act shall be selected, and such person shall act accordingly until a President or Vice President shall have qualified.

Section 4. The Congress may by law provide for the case of the death of any of the persons from whom the House of Representatives may choose a President whenever the right of choice shall have devolved upon them, and for the case of the death of any of the persons from whom the Senate may choose a Vice President whenever the right of choice shall have devolved upon them.

Section 5. Sections 1 and 2 shall take effect on the 15th day of October following the ratification of this article.

Section 6. This article shall be inoperative unless it shall have been ratified as an amendment to the Constitution by the legislatures of three-fourths of the several States within seven years from the date of its submission.

ARTICLE XXI

Passed by Congress February 20, 1933   Ratified December 5, 1933

Section 1. The eighteenth article of amendment to the Constitution of the United States is hereby repealed.

Section 2. The transportation or importation into any State, Territory, or possession of the United States for delivery or use therein of intoxicating liquors in violation of the laws thereof, is hereby prohibited.

Section 3. This article shall be inoperative unless it shall have been ratified as an amendment to the Constitution by conventions in the several States, as provided in the Constitution, within seven years from the date of the submission thereof to the States by the Congress.

ARTICLE XXII

Passed by Congress March 12, 1947   Ratified February 26, 1951

Section 1. No person shall be elected to the office of the President more than twice, and no person who has held the office of President, or acted as President, for more than two years of a term to which some other person was elected President shall be elected to the office of the President more than once.

But this article shall not apply to any person holding the office of President when this article was proposed by the Congress, and shall not prevent any person who may be holding the office of President, or acting as President, during the term within which this article becomes operative from holding the office of President or acting as President during the remainder of such term.

Section 2. This article shall be inoperative unless it shall have been ratified as an amendment to the Constitution by the legislatures of three fourths of the several States within seven years from the date of its submission to the States by the Congress.

ARTICLE XXIII

Passed by Congress June 16, 1960   Ratified March 29, 1961

Section 1. The District constituting the seat of Government of the United States shall appoint in such manner as the Congress may direct:

A number of electors of President and Vice President equal to the whole number of Senators and Representatives in Congress to which the District would be entitled if it were a State, but in no event more than the least populous state; they shall be in addition to those appointed by the states, but shall be considered, for the purpose of the election of President and Vice President, to be electors appointed by a State; and they shall meet in the District and perform such duties as provided by the twelfth article of amendment.

Section 2. The Congress shall have power to enforce this article by appropriate legislation.

ARTICLE XXIV

Passed by Congress August 27, 1962   Ratified January 23, 1964

Section 1. The right of citizens of the United States to vote in any primary or other election for President or Vice President, for electors for President or Vice President, or for Senator or Representative in Congress, shall not be denied or abridged by the United States or any State by reason of failure to pay any poll tax or other tax.

Section 2. The Congress shall have the power to enforce this article by appropriate legislation.

ARTICLE XXV

Passed by Congress July 6, 1965   Ratified February 10, 1967

Section 1. In case of the removal of the President from office or his death or resignation, the Vice President shall become President.

Section 2. Whenever there is a vacancy in the office of the Vice President, the President shall nominate a Vice President who shall take the office upon confirmation by a majority vote of both houses of Congress.

Section 3. Whenever the President transmits to the President pro tempore of the Senate and the Speaker of the House of Representatives his written declaration that he is unable to discharge the powers and duties of his office, and until he transmits to them a written declaration to the contrary, such powers and duties shall be discharged by the Vice President as Acting President.

Section 4. Whenever the Vice President and a majority of either the principal officers of the executive departments or of such other body as Congress may by law provide, transmit to the President pro tempore of the Senate and the Speaker of the House of Representatives their written declaration that the President is unable to discharge the powers and duties of his office, the Vice President shall immediately assume the powers and duties of the office as Acting President.

Thereafter, when the President transmits to the President pro tempore of the Senate and the Speaker of the House of Representatives his written declaration that no inability exists, he shall resume the powers and duties of his office unless the Vice President and a majority of either the principal officers of the executive department or of such other body as Congress may by law provide, transmit within four days to the President pro tempore of the Senate and the Speaker of the House of Representatives their written declaration that the President is unable to discharge the powers and duties of his office. Thereupon Congress shall decide the issue, assembling within 48 hours if not in session. If the Congress, within 21 days after receipt of the latter written declaration, or, if Congress is not in session, within 21 days after Congress is required to assemble, determines by two-thirds vote of both houses that the President is unable to discharge the powers and duties of his office, the Vice President shall continue to discharge the same as Acting President; otherwise, the President shall resume the powers and duties of his office.

LESSON SEVEN

PUPILS' GUIDE

The National Archives

I. Suggestions for Study

    a)   Read the Lesson material carefully.

    b)   Look up Philadelphia, Pennsylvania; and Washington, D.C. on your United States map at home.

II. Lesson Material

    Text: Lesson 7 - The National Archives.

III. 1. The kind of Nation that America is:

    i)   The statue *Heritage*, in front of the National Archives depicts the government's role in defending: (Circle one)

        a)   Health programs

        b)   Sports activities

        c)   The Sanctity of the Home and Family

        d)   School Counsellors

    ii)   The Seal of the National Archives portrays, in predominance: (Circle one)

        a)   The Code of Hammurabi

        b)   The Koran

        c)   A Menorah

        d)   The Ten Commandments (Exodus 20)

    iii)   In the Seal of the National Archives, to the right of the Ten Commandments, stand: (Fill in the blanks)

        a)   "_____" and "_____," symbolizing our _____ and _____ system of government and showing forth from whence_____ _____ is derived.

    iv)   Upon entering the Main Rotunda of the National Archives, one is greeted by two large murals, entitled: (Circle two)

        a)   Japanese Cherry Blossoms

        b)   The Magna Carta

c) The Declaration of Independence (July 4, 1776)
d) "American Originals"
e) World War II
f) The U.S. Constitution (September 17, 1787)

v) These two famous mural paintings are the workmanship of: (Circle one)

a) A Hindu artist
b) A disciple of Buddha
c) New York's Barry Faulkner
d) Mao Tse Tung

vi) The National Archives was completed in 1937. When were these paintings completed and displayed upon the walls of the Main Rotunda? (Circle one)

a) 1976
b) 1930's
c) 1987
d) 1945, during the 2nd World War

vii) The Main Rotunda of the National Archives houses three items of great value and significance to all Americans. They are: (Circle three)

a) The Dresden Collection
b) The Declaration of Independence
c) The Vatican Library
d) The French Culture Exhibit
e) The U.S. Constitution
f) The U.S. Bill of Rights

viii) The Declaration of Independence, forerunner of our U.S. Constitution, is founded upon: (Consult your text and fill in the blanks)

a) The _____ of _____. Composed by _____ _____, it begins with an _____ that man's _____ and _____ was bestowed upon him by_____ _____.

ix) The following lines are to be found in the Declaration of Independence: (Fill in the blanks)

a) We hold_____ _____ to be_____, that _____ _____ are_____ equal, that they are_____ by their _____ with certain _____ rights, that among these are _____, _____ and the _____ of happiness. . . appealing to the _____ _____ of the world, . . . declare, That these _____ _____ are, and of right ought to be, _____ and_____ states . . . And for the support of this _____, with a firm _____ on the _____ of _____ _____, we mutually_____ to each other our _____, our _____ and our _____ _____.

x) The Declaration of Independence was signed on July 4th, 1776 by John Hancock, President, by order and in behalf of the Congress. How many members of Congress, (including John Hancock) were represented in this signing? (Circle one)

    a)   20
    b)   36
    c)   56
    d)   39

xi) How many grievances against the reigning, tyrannical power, were cited in this famous American document? (Circle one)

    a)   5
    b)   10
    c)   15
    d)   27

xii) Article I, Section 1, of the *U.S. Constitution* states: (Fill in the blanks)

    a)   All legislative _____ herein granted shall be vested in a _____ of the _____ _____, which shall _____ of a _____ and _____ of _____.

xiii) Article VII of the U.S. Constitution states that: (Fill in the blanks)

    a)   The_____ of the_____ of _____ States shall be _____ for the _____ of this _____ between the States so _____ the same.

xiv) The *U.S. Constitution* was ratified, and signed by George Washington in Independence Hall, Philadelphia on September 17, 1787. It concludes thus: (Fill in the blanks)

    a)   Done in _____ by the _____ consent of the _____ present the _____ day of _____ in the year of _____ _____ [Jesus Christ] one thousand _____ hundred and _____, and of the _____ of the _____ _____ of America the _____. In _____whereof we have hereunto _____ our _____.

                             George Washington

xv) How many signers of the *U.S. Constitution* were there? (Circle one)

   a) 19
   b) 42
   c) 39
   d) 27

xvi) What are two other names commonly given to Article I of the *U.S. Bill of Rights*? (Circle two)

   a) The Federalist clause
   b) The First Amendment clause
   c) Shay's Rebellion clause
   d) The Establishment clause

xvii) What is the first priority addressed by Congress in Article I of the *U.S. Bill of Rights*? (Circle two)

   a) Freedom of speech
   b) Peaceful assembly
   c) Prohibiting the establishment of a government, state-controlled church
   d) Petition for redress of grievances
   e) Banning any law prohibiting freedom of denominational worship

2. **Christian Character Traits:**

   Select 10 Christian virtues, values and morals inherent in the *Declaration of Independence*, the *U.S. Constitution* and the *U.S. Bill of Rights*. List them below:

   a. _____   f. _____

   b. _____   g. _____

   c. _____   h. _____

   d. _____   i. _____

   e. _____   j. _____

IV. Illustrate your work with pictures, outline map, models and drawings.

V. Memory verse:

   Unless the Lord builds the house, its builders labor in vain. Unless the Lord watches over the city, the watchmen stand guard in vain.   Psalm 127:1

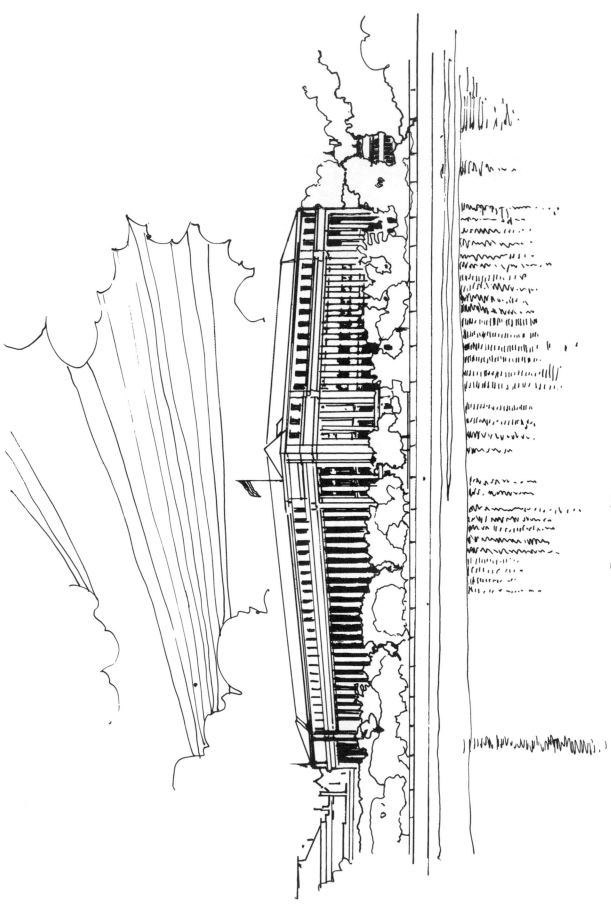

Bureau of Engraving and Printing

The Christian Heritage Of Our Nation - History Curriculum

Bureau of Engraving and Printing.

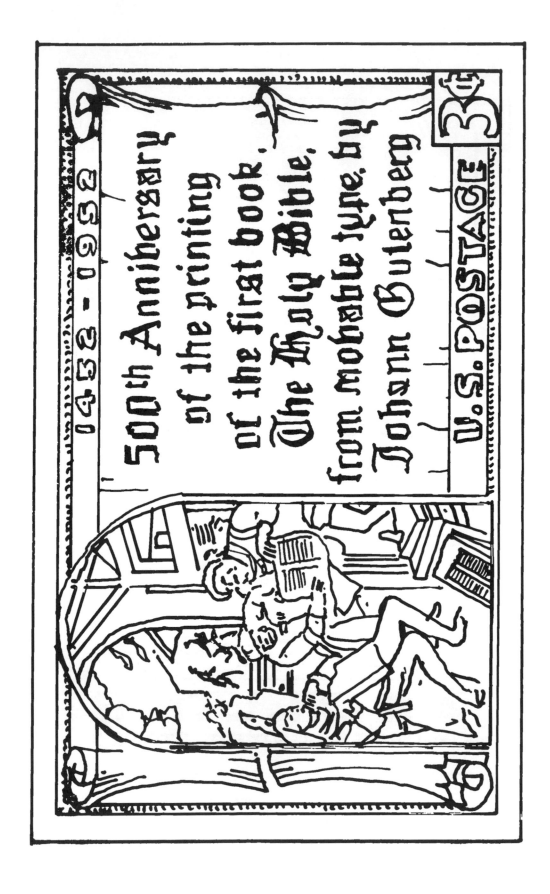

Bureau of Engraving and Printing.

Christmas **13c**

Copley, Boston Museum. USA

Bureau of Engraving and Printing.

Bureau of Engraving and Printing.

The Christian Heritage Of Our Nation - History Curriculum

Bureau of Engraving and Printing.

Bureau of Engraving and Printing.

The Christian Heritage Of Our Nation - History Curriculum

Bureau of Engraving and Printing.

LESSON 8

THE BUREAU OF ENGRAVING AND PRINTING

1864 marked the year for a recommendation of the establishment of an Engraving and Printing Bureau of the Treasury Department. Four short years later, with passage of the Act of March 3, 1869, "The Engraving and Printing Bureau" came into being. By the year 1877, all U.S. currency, its principal product, was printed in this bureau.

Portraits of three great First Officers of our nation, each of whom exemplified the Christian principles upon which this country was founded, appear upon the $1, $2 and $5 notes. They are: Washington, Jefferson and Lincoln, respectively. Another important personage, whose face appears upon the $10 note, is Alexander Hamilton. He was the first Secretary of the Treasury and, while in Philadelphia, attended Christ Church - "the nation's church." It should also be noted that our coins glorify God with the motto, *In God We Trust.*

"In God We Trust"

The following correspondence addressed to Hon. S.P. Chase, Secretary of the Treasury, and dated November 13, 1861, reveals how even our coins came to be symbolic of our Christian heritage:

Dear Sir:

You are about to submit your annual report to Congress respecting the affairs of the national finances.

One fact touching our currency has hitherto been seriously overlooked. I mean the recognition of the Almighty God in some form on our coins.

You are probably a Christian. What if our Republic were now shattered beyond reconstruction? Would not the antiquaries of succeeding centuries rightly reason from our past that we were a heathen nation? What I propose is that . . .we shall have next inside the 13 stars a ring inscribed with the words "perpetual union,". . .beneath this. . .the American flag, bearing in its field stars equal to the number of the States united; in the folds of the bars the words "God, liberty, law."

This would make a beautiful coin, to which no possible citizen could object. This would relieve us from the ignominy of heathenism. This would place us openly under the Divine protection we have personally claimed. From my heart I have felt our national shame in disowning God as not the least of our present national disasters.

To you first I address a subject that must be agitated.

(Sgd) M.R. Watkinson
Minister of the Gospel
Ridleyville, PA.[51]

A few days after reading its contents, the Secretary of the Treasury addressed his response to the Director of the Mint in Philadelphia, as follows:

Dear Sir:

No nation can be strong except in the strength of God or safe except in His defense. The trust of our people in God should be declared on our national coins.

You will cause a device to be prepared without unnecessary delay with a motto expressing in the fewest and tersest words possible this national recognition.

Yours truly,
(Sgd). S.P. Chase

A further letter from the Secretary of the Treasury to James Pollock, director of the Mint, dated December 9, 1863, finalizes the conviction that our nation's strength lies in Almighty God and His defense.

He writes:

I approve your mottoes, only suggesting that on that with the Washington obverse the motto should begin with the word "Our," so as to read:

"Our God and our Country." And on that with the shield, it should be changed so as to read: "In God we Trust." [53]

Thus it was that by Act of Congress, dated March 3, 1865, *In God we Trust* was inscribed upon our United States coins; later to be inscribed upon paper currency. The truth of its poignant message is a daily reminder to Americans where our allegiance lies: upon Almighty God and His providence (blessings) upon our land.

Another important function of the Bureau is the production of postage stamps for the United States Postal Service. Designations, such as the "Americana Series" of 1975; the "Prominent Americans Series" of 1965; the "Liberty Series" of 1954 and the "Presidential Series" of 1938, are often used for these. The function of Memorial stamps is to honour great people of caliber; worthwhile achievements; anniversaries, expositions and historical events of great significance.

The National Philatelic Collection (housed in the National Museum of American History) comprises 15 million specimens of stamps, seals and related objects. Among this formidable acquisition of items pertaining to postage, are stamps and seals with biblical themes, quotations and personages.

The Gutenberg Bible stamp, issued in 1952, commemorates the 500th anniversary of the printing of the first book, the Holy Bible, from movable type, by Johann Gutenberg. Pictured on the stamp is Gutenberg showing his proof to the Elector of Mainz.

Another famous stamp portrays George Washington taking the oath of office with his hand upon the Bible. This takes place in Federal Hall, New York City. On May 5th, 1969, a unique postage stamp was issued. It commemorates the Apollo 8 mission which first put men into orbit around the moon. Colonel Frank Borman, Captain James Lovell and Major William Anders were the astronauts on this lunar expedition. For the first time in history, the Word of God was relayed back to planet earth from the moon. A photograph taken from the moon entitled *Earthrise*, is featured on this stamp. Captioned beneath the rising earth are the first four words of Genesis, Scripture that was read from the moon to the earth: "In the beginning God. . ." (Gen. 1:1). Under the subsection "Biblical Personages" a 1983 issue of Martin Luther commemorates the 500th anniversary of this great Reformer.

July 16, 1969 saw the 200th anniversary of the settlement of California. To commemorate this historical event, a stamp was issued. It portrays the Carmel Mission belfry, with bells joyfully pealing out the good news of eternal life through faith in Christ. Another stamp shows Washington at Valley Forge on his knees, praying. It was taken from a painting by J.C. Leyendecker. Many of the stamps are from lithographs of famous paintings displayed in the National Galley of Art. Among these are: "The Adoration of the Shepherds" by Giorgione, "The Annunciation," by fifteenth century Flemish painter, Jan van Eyck; "The Small Cowper Madonna," by Raphael and "The Madonna and Child with Cherubim" by Andrea della Robbia. The 1976 Christmas issue reflects a magnificent nativity scene by John Singleton Copley. Its original can be seen in Boston's Museum of Fine Arts.

Of unusual vintage is a Christmas stamp showing the *Dove of Peace* weather-vane atop Mount Vernon, home of George Washington. A dove holds an olive branch in its beak. This comes from Genesis Chapter 8, and was ordered for Mount Vernon by George Washington himself, from Joseph Rakestraw of Philadelphia, in 1787. *Peace on Earth*! the inscription reads.

LESSON EIGHT

PUPILS' GUIDE

Bureau of Engraving and Printing

I. Suggestions for Study

a)   Read the Lesson material carefully.

b)   Look up Washington D.C.; Mount Vernon, Virginia; Charlottesville, Virginia; Springfield, Illinois and Mainz, Germany, on your map of the world at home.

II. Lesson Material

Text: Lesson 8 - The Bureau of Engraving and Printing.

III. 1.   *The kind of Nation that America is:*

i)   The Bureau of Engraving and Printing is a branch of: (Circle one)

    a)   The White House
    b)   The Treasury Department
    c)   The U.S. Capitol
    d)   The U.S. Supreme Court

ii)   What is the name of the founding father who became First Secretary of the Treasury, and what church did he attend? (Circle one)

    a)   George Washington, Pohick Episcopal Church, Virginia
    b)   Benjamin Franklin, Christ Church, Philadelphia
    c)   Alexander Hamilton, Christ Church, Philadelphia
    d)   John Adams, Old Pine Street Presbyterian Church, Philadelphia

iii)   What is the function of Memorial Stamps? (Fill in the blanks)

    a)   The function of Memorial Stamps is to _____ great _____ of _____; worthwhile _____; _____, expositions and _____ events of great _____.

iv)   Name four famous events memorialized in Commemorative stamps issued by our national Bureau of Engraving and Printing: (Circle four)

    a)   The little toy Train
    b)   A tree Ornament
    c)   The Gutenberg Bible, 1952

d) The Bugler
e) "Earthrise," 1969
f) A Runner
g) Martin Luther, 1983
h) The Dove of Peace (Genesis 8)

v) Where was our first president inaugurated into office, and what did his left hand rest upon while taking the oath of office? (Circle one)

a) The U.S. Capitol, Washington, D.C.; Map of the city
b) Independence Hall, Philadelphia; "The Immortal Mentor"
c) Federal Hall, New York; The Holy Bible
d) Nassau Hall, Princeton; Pilgrim's Progress

vi) A unique Commemorative Postage Stamp, *Earthrise*, was issued on May 5, 1969. It memorializes: (Consult your text and fill in the blanks)

a) The _____ _____ mission which first put _____ into _____ around the _____. Colonel _____ _____, Captain _____ _____ and Major _____ _____ were the _____ on this _____ expedition. For the first time in _____, the _____ of _____ was relayed back to _____ _____ from the_____.

vii) Captioned beneath the photograph *Earthrise* is inscribed: (Circle one)

a) We did it, again
b) Hoorah for the U.S.A.!
c) Protect the environment
d) In the beginning God . . .(Genesis 1:1)

viii) The National Philatelic Collection comprises numerous specimens of stamps, seals and related objects. How many are there? (Circle one)

a) 5 billion
b) 15 million
c) 20 million
d) 2 million

ix) A July 16, 1969 postage stamp commemorating the 200th anniversary of the settlement of California, portrays: (Circle one)

a) The Gold Rush in California
b) Urbanization and Development
c) The Carmel (Christian) Mission belfry
d) Rural farmlands

x) *The Dove of Peace* weathervane on the Christmas stamp comes from: (Circle one)

   a)   The Toy Museum
   b)   The Christmas Store
   c)   George and Martha Washington's home, Mount Vernon
   d)   A Brass foundry

xi) An unbroken American Christian tradition to this day, is the annual Christmas Stamp issued each Christmas. In 1976, a Great Master artist's painting of the birth of Jesus Christ, the Messiah and Savior of the world, is portrayed. The artist's name is: (Circle one)

   a)   Giorgione
   b)   John Singleton Copley
   c)   Andrea della Robbia
   d)   Raphael

xii) What phrase consistently appears upon America's paper currency? (Circle one)

   a)   Hail, Columbia
   b)   Liberty and Justice
   c)   E Pluribus Unum
   d)   In God we Trust

xiii) Who was the originator of this phrase, and in what year? (Circle one)

   a)   Joseph Rakestraw, 1787
   b)   M.R. Watkinson, Minister of the Gospel, 1861
   c)   Chester Arthur, 1884
   d)   Abraham Lincoln, 1865

xiv) Who officially authorized the inscription of this phrase upon United States coins, and in what year? (Circle one)

   a)   Salmon P. Chase, 1863
   b)   Abraham Lincoln, 1861
   c)   William Howard Taft, 1910
   d)   John Adams, 1825

xv) In whom do we, as Americans, place our trust, every time we exchange monetary notes? (Circle one)

   a)   George Washington
   b)   Thomas Jefferson

c)   Almighty God of the Bible

d)   Abraham Lincoln

2. *Christian Character Traits:*

Select 10 Christian virtues, values and morals woven into the Great Master artists' engravings, portraits and paintings reproduced by our national Bureau of Engraving and Printing. List them below:

a. _____   f. _____

b. _____   g. _____

c. _____   h. _____

d. _____   i. _____

e. _____   j. _____

IV. *Illustrate your work with pictures, outline map, models and drawings.*

V.   *Memory verse:*

In the beginning God created the heavens and the earth. And the earth was formless and void, and darkness was over the surface of the deep; and the Spirit of God was moving over the surface of the waters. Then God said, "Let there be light;" and there was light. And God saw that the light was good; and God separated the light from the darkness. (Genesis1:1-4)

The Organization of American States

Queen Isabel of Spain – The Organization of American States

Daniel the Prophet
The Organization of American States

LESSON 9

THE ORGANIZATION OF AMERICAN STATES

President Theodore Roosevelt laid the cornerstone to this building in 1908. Three-quarters of its cost was a gift of philanthropist Andrew Carnegie. Two years later, in April, 1910, the site was dedicated as the International Headquarters of the Organization of American States. The purpose and function of the Organization of American States is the establishment and maintenance of a forum for the peaceful co-habitation of nations in the western hemisphere. The handsome edifice, its outer facade constructed of white Georgian marble, was primarily designed to resemble a Spanish colonial mansion, but includes English, French, Portuguese and American streams of architecture. The sculptured groupings to either side of the main entrance-way represent South America to the left and North America to the right. The latter is a work of art executed by the sculptor of Mount Rushmore in South Dakota, Gutzon Borglum.[54]

Daniel the Prophet (the statue of)

An exact granite replica of the original stands beneath the branches of a tall evergreen tree on the front lawn. Its original stone model, executed by Brazilian sculptor Antonio Francisco Lisboa (1730-1814) stands in Ouro Preto, Brazil. He was a much-loved artist, affectionately known as "Aleijadinho," meaning, "the crippled one." Daniel stands alone—placid and calm—with a lion at his feet. To the side of the statue an inscribed scroll indicates Daniel's identity as Old Testament prophet of God, who predicted the four Great World Empires and the seven years' Great Tribulation.[55]

Isabel of Spain (the statue of)

The regal life-size statue of Isabella of Spain, who provided the financial means so that Christopher Columbus could accomplish his voyage of discovery to the unknown west, stands sentinel directly in the foreground of the building. Spanish sculptor Jose Luis Sanchez made the bronze cast by the process of "lost wax." Its style is original and contemporary. Isabella holds a pomegranate in her hands, from which a dove, symbol of the Holy Spirit, takes flight. A bronze plaque upon the base of the statue reads:

> This is the statue of Queen Isabella of Spain and the Americas who sent Christopher Columbus to discover the New World. Donated by Spain to the Organization of American States. April 14, 1966. Day of the Americas.

This extraordinary work of art, dedicated on April 14, 1966, was a gift of the Institute of Hispanic Culture in Madrid.[56]

The Christian Heritage Of Our Nation - History Curriculum

LESSON NINE

PUPILS' GUIDE

The Organization of American States

I. Suggestions for Study

    a)   Read the Lesson material carefully.

    b)   Look up South America; Spain; Israel and Babylon on your map of the world at home.

II. Lesson Material

    Text: Lesson 9 - The Organization of American States.

III. 1. The Kind of Nation that America is:

    i)   The sculptured grouping to the right of the Main Entranceway of the Organization of American States represents North America. It is the work of famous Great Master sculptor: (Circle one)

        a)   Leonardo da Vinci (Italian)

        b)   Gutzon Borglum (American)

        c)   Jean Antoine Houdon (French)

        d)   Jose Luis Sanchez (Spanish)

    ii)   Who laid the cornerstone to the Organization of American States, and when? (Circle one)

        a)   Chester Arthur, 1883

        b)   Abraham Lincoln, 1865

        c)   Theodore Roosevelt, 1908

        d)   Harry Truman, 1945

    iii)   Who funded two-thirds of this edifice: (Circle one)

        a)   The French government

        b)   The Spanish Monarchy

        c)   The Organization of South American States

        d)   American philanthropist, Andrew Carnegie

iv) What is the purpose and function of the Organization of American States? (Consult text and fill in the blanks)

   a) The purpose and function of the Organization of American States is the _____ and _____ of a _____ for the _____ _____ of nations in the _____ _____.

v) A replica of a famous stone statue stands on the front lawn of the Organization of American States. It depicts: (Circle one)

   a) An Inca king
   b) A Mayan idol
   c) Daniel, the Old Testament prophet of God
   d) A totem pole

vi) A scroll on the side of this statue indicates: (Fill in the blanks)

   a) _____ identity as ____ _____ prophet of _____ who predicted the _____ _____ _____ _____ and the _____ years' _____ _____.

vii) The life-size bronze statue in front of the Organization of American States is that of: (Circle one)

   a) Jose Artigas of Uruguay
   b) Don Quixote
   c) Santa Ana
   d) Queen Isabel of Spain

viii) What does the life-size bronze statue in front of the Organization of American States hold in its hands? (Fill in the blanks)

   a) _____ holds a _____ in _____ _____, from which a _____, symbol of the _____ _____, takes flight.

ix) Describe the purpose and meaning for this life-size bronze statue placed directly in front of the Organization of American States. (Consult text and fill in the blanks)

   a) This is the _____ of _____ _____ of Spain and the _____ who sent _____ _____ to discover the _____ _____. _____ by Spain to the _____ of _____ States. April 14, 1966. Day of the _____.

x)   Who enabled Christopher Columbus to accomplish his voyage of discovery to the unknown west? (Circle one)

   a)   The Italian government
   b)   Pope Alexander VII
   c)   The Portugese monarchy
   d)   Queen Isabel of Spain, a Christian

2. *Christian Character Traits:*

Select 10 Christian virtues, values and morals woven into the art, sculpture and inscriptions pertaining to the Organization of American States. List them below:

a.   _____   f.   _____

b.   _____   g.   _____

c.   _____   h.   _____

d.   _____   i.   _____

e.   _____   j.   _____

IV. *Illustrate your work with pictures, outline map, models and drawings.*

V. *Memory verse:*

Alas, O Lord, the great and awesome God, who keeps His covenant and lovingkindness for those who love Him and keep His commandments, we have sinned, committed iniquity, acted wickedly, and rebelled, even turning aside from Thy commandments and ordinances. Moreover, we have not listened to Thy servants the prophets, who spoke in Thy name to our kings, our princes, our fathers, and all the people of the land. Righteousness belongs to Thee, O Lord, but to us, open shame.

Daniel 9:4b-7a

The John F. Kennedy Center for the Performing Arts

The Christian Heritage Of Our Nation - History Curriculum

After "The First Day of Creation" Aubusson Tapestry by John Coburn

After "The Second Day of Creation" Aubusson Tapestry by John Coburn

After "The Third Day of Creation," Aubusson Tapestry by John Coburn

After "The Fourth Day of Creation" Aubusson Tapestry by John Coburn

The Christian Heritage Of Our Nation - History Curriculum

After "The Fifth Day of Creation" Aubusson Tapestry by John Coburn

After "The Sixth Day of Creation" Aubusson Tapestry by John Coburn

The Christian Heritage Of Our Nation - History Curriculum

After "The Seventh Day of Creation" Aubusson Tapestry by John Coburn

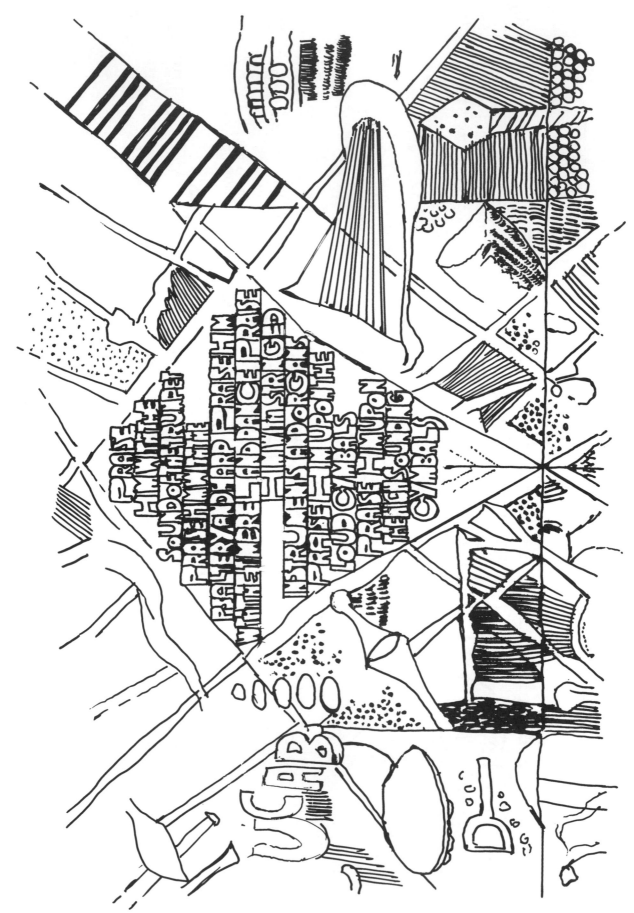

Psalm 150 - West Wall, Israeli Lounge, John F. Kennedy Center for the Performing Arts.

The Christian Heritage Of Our Nation - History Curriculum

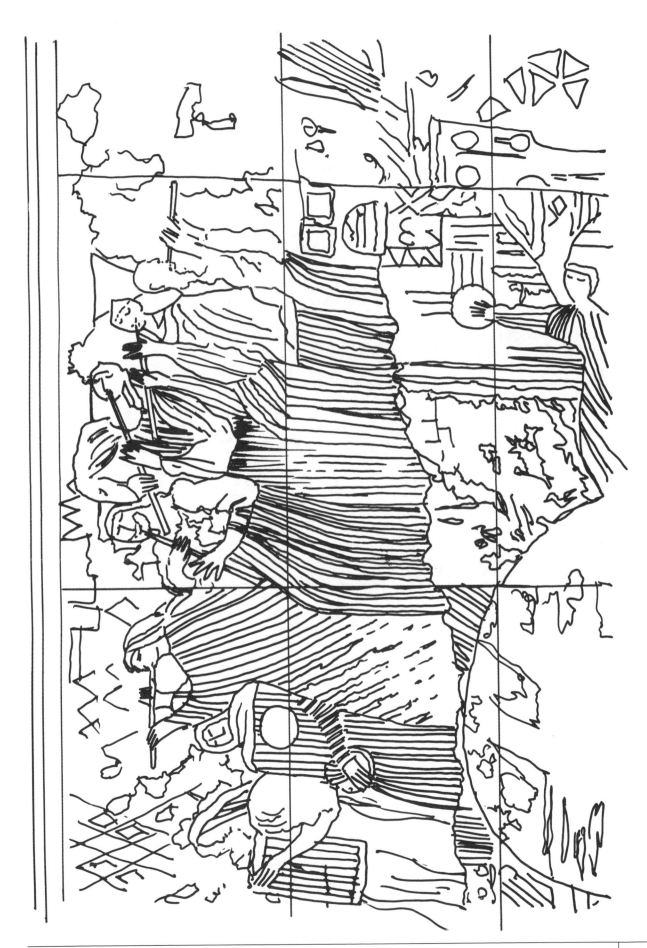

The Israelites play Musical Instruments to the glory of God - Psalm 81, Ceiling of the Israeli Lounge - John F. Kennedy Center for the Performing Arts.

King David plays the Harp. Psalm 81 portrayed upon the Ceiling - Israeli Lounge,
John F. Kennedy Center for the Performing Arts.

The Christian Heritage Of Our Nation - History Curriculum

*Miriam dances and plays the Tambourines. Psalm 81- Ceiling of the Israeli Lounge,
John F. Kennedy Center for the Performing Arts.*

The Israelites sing Hymns of Praise to Jehovah God. Psalm 81 -
Ceiling of the Israeli Lounge, John F. Kennedy Center for the Performing Arts.

Joshua and his followers blow Rams' Horns as they encircle the Walls of Jericho.
Psalm 81 - Ceiling of the Israeli Lounge, John F. Kennedy Center for the Performing Arts.

LESSON TEN

THE JOHN F. KENNEDY CENTER
FOR THE PERFORMING ARTS

Too often in the past, we have thought of the artist as an idler and a dillettante and of the lover of arts as somehow sissy or effete. We have done both an injustice. The life of the artist is, in relation to his work, stern and lonely. He has labored hard, often amid deprivation, to perfect his skill. He has turned aside from quick success in order to strip his vision of everything secondary or cheapening. His working life is marked by intense application and intense discipline.[57]

John F. Kennedy, President, United States of America

A report submitted to the House of Representatives on December 17, 1963, in conjunction with the John F. Kennedy Center Act, incorporated ideals held by the 35th President of the United States:

Nothing was more characteristic of President John F. Kennedy than his support of the arts in America. . .He believed that through its artists, its poets, musicians, painters, dramatists—a society expressed its highest values.[58]

In 1964 a bill to establish a living national memorial to John F. Kennedy was signed by President Johnson and passed by Congress. It was thus that the modern, square edifice designed by architect Edward Durrell Stone and constructed entirely of white Carrara marble, gift of Italy, came into being. The center opened its doors to the public on September 8, 1971, celebrating the world premiere of Leonard Bernstein's solemn "Mass."

A 45-member Board of Trustees, 30 of whom are appointed by the President of the United States for ten-year terms, sets and directs all performing arts policies. There are three main theaters on the ground floor. They comprise the Eisenhower Theater, with approximately 1,100 seats; the Opera House, seating 2,200 persons, and the Concert Hall, with a capacity for 2,700 people. The Concert Hall stage was a special gift of schoolchildren in memory of John Phillip Sousa, beloved American composer.

A Bicentennial gift to the Center from Japan, the Terrace Theater on the Roof Level of the building accommodates 500 theatergoers.

Two main entranceways lead into *The Hall of Nations* and *The Hall of States*, which show forth flags in colorful array from the ceiling above. Represented here, respectively, are the 138 nations maintaining diplomatic relations with the United States; and flags of our fifty states in the Union, together with those of Puerto Rico, the Virgin Islands, Guam, American Samoa and the District of Columbia.

The red-carpeted Grand Foyer spans a length of six hundred and thirty feet, competing favorably with the Washington Monument in height. Eighteen Orrefors crystal chandeliers, each weighing a ton, dazzle the onlooker. They were a gift of Sweden. Sixty-feet tall Belgian mirrors line the inner walls, reflecting further the resplendent glitter of this Performing Arts Hallway.

In the center of the foyer, an unusual bronze rendition of Kennedy's head greets the eye. Sculptor Robert Berks has captivated the poise and life-like facial expressions of his subject. It is said that Kennedy's profile betrays a smile on the one hand, and sadness on the other.

A gift of the State of Israel, the Israeli Lounge was dedicated on November 30, 1971. No less than forty-eight musical instruments mentioned in the Old Testament are displayed upon its walls. The visitor is overwhelmed by an exciting and colourful biblical panorama. A masterpiece of both literal and symbolic interpretation, Psalms 81 and 150 orchestrate their own praises to Jehovah God through the artists' skillful expression upon wall and ceiling.[59]

Splendid royal blues and reds painted upon forty panels in the ceiling depict Shraga Weil's interpretation of Psalm 81:

> Sing for joy to God our strength
> Shout joyfully to the God of Jacob
> Raise a song, strike the timbrel
> The sweet sounding lyre with the harp
> Blow the trumpet at the new moon
> At the full moon on our feast-day
> For it is a statute for Israel
> An ordinance for the God of Jacob[60]

Portrayed upon these panels, is Joshua and his followers encircling the walls of Jericho, blowing rams' horns; David playing his harp; and Miriam dancing and playing the tambourines to celebrate the passage of the Israelites through the Red Sea.[61]

Carved from rich African walnut in bas-relief with copper and brass lettering, the entire West Wall of this lounge represents sculptor Nehemiah Azaz's rendition of the last of the Psalms, which ends in joyful praises to our God and Father:

> Praise Him with the sound of trumpet
> Praise Him with the psaltery and harp
> Praise Him with timbrel and dance
> Praise Him with stringed instruments and organs
> Praise Him upon the loud cymbals
> Praise Him upon the high sounding cymbals[62]

Seven large Aubusson tapestries entitled *The Creation* adorn the walls on the Roof Level of the Center. A gift from Australia, they were executed by John Coburn, designer of the curtains in the new Sydney Opera House. Each tapestry has a theme of its own, taken from the first chapter of Genesis and captioned with a simple phrase by the artist himself: *The First Day*: The Spirit of God brooded over the waters. *The Second Day*: God separated the light from the dark. *The Third Day*: God created the earth. *The Fourth Day*: God created the vault of the sky and He made the sun and the moon and the stars to shed their light on the earth. *The Fifth Day*: God created the fish of the sea, the birds of the air and the beasts of the dry land. *The Sixth Day*: God created men. *The Seventh Day*: God rested.[63]

Each Christmas sees Handel's majestic and awe-inspiring *Messiah* performed by the National Symphony Orchestra, with Mistislav Rostropovitch as its conductor. The Choral Arts Society adds its own compositions to this rich heritage of Christmas music glorifying Christ.

LESSON TEN

PUPILS' GUIDE

The John F. Kennedy Center
for the Performing Arts

I. Suggestions for Study

a) Read the lesson material carefully.
b) Look up the Middle East and Australia on your map of the world at home.

II. Lesson Material

The Holy Bible (King James Version).
Text: Lesson 10 - The John F. Kennedy Center for the Performing Arts.

III. 1. The kind of Nation that America is:

i)   What is the name of the artist/designer of *The Creation* Tapestries in our National Performing Arts Center? (Circle one)

a)   Mikhael Baryshnikof
b)   Leonard Bernstein
c)   Rostropovitch
d)   John Coburn

ii) What is the Great Master artist's caption for *The Fourth Day* of Creation Tapestry? (Fill in the blanks)

a)   On the Fourth Day,_____ created the vault of the_____, and He made the_____, and the_____, and the _____ to shed their _____ upon the _____.

iii) What is the Great Master artist's caption for *The Fifth Day* of Creation Tapestry? (Fill in the blanks)

a)   On the Fifth Day_____ created the_____ of the _____, the _____ of the ____ and the _____ of the dry _____.

iv) What is the Great Master artist's caption for *The Sixth Day* of Creation Tapestry? (Fill in the blanks)

a)   On the Sixth Day,_____created_____.

v) What is the Great Master artist's caption for *The Seventh Day* of Creation Tapestry? (Fill in the blanks)

    a)   On the Seventh Day,_____ _____.

vi) What does the Holy Bible tell us about the very beginning of the universe and creation? (Look up Genesis 1:1 in your Bible)

    a)   In the beginning, _____ created _____ _____ and _____ _____. (Genesis 1:1)

vii) Fill in all of the things God created or did on each Day of Creation in the Great Master artist's *The Creation* Tapestries in our National Performing Arts Center:

    a)   *The First Day* _____

    b)   *The Second Day* _____

    c)   *The Third Day* _____

    d)   *The Fourth Day* _____

    e)   *The Fifth Day* _____

    f)   *The Sixth Day* _____

    g)   *The Seventh Day* _____

viii) A report submitted to the House of Representatives on December 17, 1963 incorporated ideals held by the 35th President of the United States. What were they? (Fill in the blanks)

    a)   Nothing was more _____ of President John F. Kennedy than his _____ of the _____ in _____. . . He believed that through its _____, its_____, _____, _____, _____, a society expressed its _____ _____.

ix) There are four theaters in the John F. Kennedy Center for the Performing Arts. They comprise: (Fill in the blanks)

    a)   The _____ Theater, with approximately_____ seats; the _____ _____, with a capacity for _____ persons; the_____ _____, accommodating _____ people and the _____ _____, seating _____ theatergoers.

x) What is our national performing arts center's annual Christmas tradition, performed by the National Symphony Orchestra? (Circle one)

a) "A Wreath of Holly"
b) Holiday Greetings
c) The Messiah or "Christ the King" by Handel
d) Happy Hanukkah

xi) How many Old Testment musical instruments are portrayed upon the walls of the Israeli Lounge? (Circle one)

a) 20
b) 35
c) 81
d) 48

xii) Which of the Psalms are depicted upon the walls and ceiling of the Israeli Lounge? (Circle two)

a) Psalm 24
b) Psalm 81
c) Psalm 125
d) Pslam 144
e) Psalm 150

xiii) Two foremost Israeli artists were chosen to execute these artistic reenactments of Biblical truths and praises to Almighty God. They are: (Circle two)

a) Bezalel
b) Nehemiah Azaz
c) Oholiab
d) Shraga Weil

xiv) The Israeli artist's interpretation of Psalm 81, depicted upon the ceiling of the Israeli Lounge, reads as follows: (Fill in the blanks)

a) _____
    _____
    _____
    _____
    _____
    _____
    _____
    _____

xv) The Israeli artist's rendition of Psalm 150, depicted upon the West Wall of the Israeli Lounge, reads as follows: (Fill in the blanks)

a) _____

_____

_____

_____

_____

_____

2. Christian Character Traits:

Select 10 Christian virtues, values and morals woven into the art, sculpture and inscriptions of the John F. Kennedy Center for the Performing Arts. List them below:

a. _____ f. _____

b. _____ g. _____

c. _____ h. _____

d. _____ i. _____

e. _____ j. _____

IV. Illustrate your work with pictures, outline map, models and drawings.

V. Memory Verses:

Genesis 1:1-3; 26-27.

In the beginning God created the heavens and the earth. And the earth was formless and void, and darkness was over the surface of the deep and the Spirit of God was moving over the surface of the waters. Then God said, "Let there be light"; and there was light. . .Then God said, "Let Us make man in Our image, according to Our likeness; and let them rule over the fish of the sea and over the birds of the sky and over the cattle and over all the earth, and over every creeping thing that creeps on the earth." And God created man in his own image, in the image of God he created him; male and female He created them.

FOOTNOTES

[1] Hagner, Alexander B. *Street Nomenclature of Washington City*. Washington: 1897, p. 4.

[2] Kite, Elizabeth Sarah. *L'Enfant and Washington (1791-1792)*. Johns Hopkins Press, Baltimore, 1929.

[3] Olszewski, George J. *The History of the Mall, Washington, D.C.* U.S. Department of Interior, National Park Service.

[4] August 15, 1896. (Washington Evening Star).

[5] Olszewski, George J., *The Construction History of Union Station*. Washington, D.C.

[6] Ibid

[7] Eliot, Charles Williams. *Inscriptions over Pavilion, Union Station*, Washington, D.C. (Late President Emeritus, Harvard University).

[8] Ibid

[9] David, Maurice. *Who was Christopher Columbus?* Letter from Don Cristobal Colon to his son, Don Diego, published by the Duchess of Berwick y Alba. New York: The Research Publishing Company, 1933, p. 92.

[10] Kling, August J. "Columbus—A Layman Christ-bearer to Unchartered Isles." The Presbyterian Layman. October, 1971.

[11] Columbus, Christopher. *Concerning the Islands Lately Discovered*. The Epistle of Christopher Colon to Lord Raphael Sanxis, Treasurer of King Ferdinand of Spain. May 3, 1493. Rare Manuscript Division of Library of Congress, Washington, D.C.

[12] Columbus, Christopher. Translation of Manuscript copy of a Letter written by Christopher Columbus to the King and Queen of Spain, dated on the Island of Jamaica, July 7, 1503. Rare Manuscript Division of Library of Congress, Washington, D.C. pp. 8-10.

[13] The United States Capitol Historical Society. *We the People, the Story of the United States Capitol, its Past and its Promise*. Washington, D.C. 1978, p. 77.

[14] Ibid

[15] Ibid

[16] Documented by the Office of the Architect of the Capitol.

[17] Ibid

[18] Ibid

[19] Ibid

[20] Ibid

[21] The Architect of the Capitol under the direction of the Joint Committee on the Library. Art in the U.S. Capitol U.S.G.P.O. Washington, 1976, p. 199.

[22] House Document No. 234. 84th Congress, lst Session. *The Prayer Room in the United States Capitol* . U.S.G.P.O. Washington, 1956, p. 7.

[23] Ibid

[24] Ibid

[25] Documented by the Office of the Architect of the Capitol.

[26] Framed letter displayed in the basement of the Supreme Court (together with other historical items.) Removed since chapter was completed.

[27] Statistics on file with the Library of Congress of the United States.

[28] Documented with the Library of Congress of the United States.

[29] Engraved upon the mantel of the State Dining Room, The White House. Conger, Clement E., Curator of The White House. Letter to author. 5/3/84.

[30] Meyers, Earl Schenck. *The White House and the Presidency*. Wonder Books, New York, 1965. p. 10.

[31] Ibid

[32] Documented with the Office of the Architect of the Capitol.

[33] Ibid

[34] Published letters of Abigail Adams. (Rare Manuscript Division, Library of Congress of the United States).

[35] Ibid

[36] Documented with the Office of the Architect of the Capitol.

[37] Treasury Department, Office of the Secretary, Department Circular No. 54. Washington, April 17, 1905.

[38] Department of the Interior. National Park Service Fact Sheet.

[39] Ibid

[40] Ibid

[41] Burk, W. Herbert, B.D. *Washington's Prayers*. (Facsimile of original) Published for the benefit of Washington Memorial Chapel, Norristown, PA., 1907, pp. 37-83.

[42] Weems, Mason L. *A History of the Life and Death, Virtues and Exploits of GeorgeWashington, Esq.* faithfully taken from authentic documents, and now, in a third edition improved, respectfully offered to the perusal of his contrymen; as also, of all others who wish to see human nature in its most finished form. Reprinted by John Bioren: Philadelphia, 1800.

[43] *Washington's Addresses to the Churches*. Old South Leaflets, No. 65, 1896, pp. 1-13.

[44] Records of the Columbia Historical Society. Blair: Lafayette Square, p.154.

[45] Ibid

[46] A Tribute prepared by direction of Trustees of St. John's Church Orphanage of Washington, D.C. *Sarah Williams Huntington*. Beresford Printer, 1918.

[47] Ibid

[48] Ibid

[49] Ibid

[50] Ibid

[51] Watkinson, M.R., Minister of the Gospel to Hon. S.P. Chase, Secretary of the Treasury. November 13, 1861.

[52] Hon. S.P. Chase, Secretary of the Treasury to Director of the Mint. Philadelphia, November 20, 1861.

[53] Secretary of the Treasury to Director of the Mint. Philadelphia, December 9, 1863.

[54] *The House of the Americas in Washington, D.C.* (Information put out by the Library of the Organization of American States).

[55] *Statues in the Gardens of the Pan American Union Building.* (Library of the O.A.S.)

[56] Ibid

[57] John F. Kennedy: *Words to Remember.* (With a foreword by Robert F. Kennedy). Hallmark Editions, 1967.

[58] John F. Kennedy Center Act. 88th Congress, 1st Session. House of Representatives, December 17, 1963. Report no. 1050, Accompanying H.J. Res. 871.

[59] Documentation from the John F. Kennedy Center for the Performing Arts Library, Washington, D.C.

[60] Ibid

[61] Ibid

[62] Ibid

[63] Ibid

[64] Aldrich, George I. and Forbes, Alexander. *The Third Book,* (Stories, Rimes, Riddles) American Book Company: 1900.

ANSWERS TO QUESTIONS

LESSON 1

III.

1. i)   c

 ii)   a, b, c

 iii)   d

 iv)   a, c

 v)   d

 vi)   e

 vii)   c

 viii)   c

2. **Christian Character Traits:**

a. adherence to the Word of God
b. dependence upon God
c. prayerfulness
d. teachability through the Holy Spirit
e. singlemindedness
f. brokenness for lost souls
g. zeal for Gospel truth
h. repentence of sins
i. humility
j. gratitude to Almighty God

LESSON 2

III.

1. i)   c

 ii)   Armed America stands in the center with a spear behind her, and a shield bearing U.S.A. upon it. Beneath the shield is inscribed July 4, 1776. America gazes at Hope to the right, who beckons to her to proceed. However, America points towards Justice, to the left, who holds a pair of scales in her left hand and a scroll in her right, reading: *Constitution, 17 September, 1787.*

iii)   Without Justice, there is no hope for America, our justice being squarely based upon the Constitution, which is based upon the Declaration of Independence, which, in turn, is based upon the justice of God's words.

iv)   d

v)   To make beautiful the Capitol of the one country on earth in which there is liberty. This he did with deep gratitude to a nation he loved; a nation which had opened its arms wide to him in his hour of need.

vi)   a) Thomas Jefferson
      b, c, e, g

vii)   d

viii)   c

ix)   The financier of the American Revolution. The artist has depicted a Bible next to his elbow, opened at Matthew's Gospel, Chapter 5.

x)   c

xi)   d

xii)   d

xiii)   c

xiv)   b

xv)   Beneath the figure lost in prayer, the seal of the United States stands out, on the one hand depicting prominence and success, and on the other, subjection to its God and King.

2.   *Christian Character Traits:*

a.   prayerfulness
b.   humility
c.   obedience
d.   subjection to Almighty God
e.   singlemindedness

f.   gratitude
g.   trust in the Lord
h.   courage
i.   leadership
j.   self-sacrifice

LESSON 3

III.

1. i) a) The Contemplation of Justice
      b) The Authority of Law

   ii) The figure is enveloped in thought. The small statue she holds at her side is the symbol of justice, which indicates on what she is thinking. . .It is a realistic conception of what I consider a heroic type of person with a head and body expressive of the beauty and intelligence of justice.

   iii) c

   iv) d

   v) a) *The Power of Government* and *The Majesty of the Law*

      b) (iii)

   vi) a, d, f, j, l, n

   vii) d, g, i, k, l

   viii) c

   ix) c

   x) d

   xi) A stark reminder of the origin and basis for our American legal system is depicted in the central figure of Moses holding the two tablets of the Old Testament Law, one in either hand.

   2. Christian Character Traits:

   a. charity
   b. mercy
   c. prayerfulness
   d. peace
   e. wisdom

   f. defense of virtue
   g. justice
   h. guardianship of liberty
   i. intelligence
   j. Divine inspiration

LESSON 4

III.

1. i) *The Torch of Learning*, welcoming all who wish to delve into the vast array of knowledge which this library has to offer.

    ii) b

    iii) d

    iv) c

    v) b

    vi) b

    vii) c

    viii) c

    ix) a) Nature is the Art of God.
         b) How charming is Divine philosophy.
         c) One God, one Law, one element, one far off, Divine event, to whom the whole creation moves.
         d) What doth the Lord require of thee, but to do justly, to love mercy, and to walk humbly with thy God. (Micah 6:8)
         e) The Heavens declare the glory of God, and the firmament showeth His handiwork. (Psalm 19:1)

    x) c

    xi) More than 25 million cards, representing the largest repository of true Americanism in the world.

    xii) c

    xiii) c

    xiv) c

    xv) d

xvi) The old historic 1897 Library of Congress building is called the *Thomas Jefferson building*, because Thomas Jefferson sacrificially gave his own personal collection to Congress, consisting of 6,700 priceless volumes, at Congress' own price, to compensate for the licentious barbarism of the British.

xvii) An Israeli woman, her hands raised in prayer and praise to Almighty God. The Ten Commandments stand at her side; the scroll of the Old Testament on her lap.

2. *Christian Character Traits:*

a. humility
b. mercy
c. justice
d. servitude
e. obedience

f. prayerfulness
g. praise
h. selflessness
i. diligence
j. perseverance

LESSON 5

III.

1. i) c

ii) Joseph is a fruitful bough, even a fruitful bough by a well; whose branches run over a wall: The archers have sorely grieved him and shot at him: But his bow abode in strength, and the arms of his hands were made strong by the hands of the mighty God of Jacob; (from thence is the Shepherd, the Stone of Israel;) Even by the God of thy father, who shall help thee; and by the Almighty, who shall bless thee with blessings of heaven above . . .

iii) a

iv) c

v) a) The German Lutheran Congregation in Philadelphia.
b) The Presbyterian Church in the United States of America.
c) The Methodist Episcopal Church in the United States.
d) The United Baptist Churches in Virginia.
e) The German Reformed Congregations in the United States.
f) The Society of the United Brethren for Propagating the Gospel among

the heathen.

g) The Protestant Episcopal Church in the States of New York; New Jersey; Pennsylvania; Delaware; Maryland; Virginia and North Carolina.

h) The Reformed Dutch Church in North America.

i) The Religious Society called Quakers in Pennsylvania; New Jersey; Delaware and the Western part of Maryland and Virginia.

j) The Roman Catholics in the United States.

k) The Hebrew Congregation in Savannah.

l) The Universal Church lately assembled in Philadelphia.

m) The Congregational Church and Society at Medway, Georgia.

n) The New Church in Baltimore.

vi)   b

vii)   If I could have entertained the slightest apprehension, that the Constitution framed in the convention, where I had the honor to preside, might possibly endanger the religious rights of any ecclesiastical society, certainly I would never have placed my signature to it; . . .

viii) . . . May your devotions before the throne of grace be prevalent in calling down the blessings of Heaven upon yourselves and your country.

ix)   . . . It will be a desirable thing. . .to cooperate, . . .with the disinterested endeavours of your Society to civilize and christianize the savages of the wilderness. Under these impressions, I pray Almighty God to have you always in His holy keeping.

x)   On this occasion, it would ill become me to conceal the joy I have felt in perceiving the fraternal affection, which appears to increase every day, among the friends of genuine religion. It affords edifying prospects, indeed, to see Christians of different denominations dwell together in more charity, and conduct themselves in respect to each other with a more Christian-like spirit, than ever they have done in any former age, or in any other nation.

xi)   c

xii)   c

xiii) a, b, e, f

xiv)   d

xv)   b

xvi)   c

xvii)   I pray Heaven to bestow the best of Blessings on this House and all
that shall hereafter inhabit it. May none but Honest and Wise Men
ever Rule under this Roof.

xviii)   c

xix)   b

2.   *Christian Character Traits:*

a.   obedience
b.   prayerfulness
c.   contrition
d.   mortification
e.   self-sacrifice

f.   sincerity
g.   gratitude
h.   honesty
i.   confession of sins
j.   wisdom

LESSON 6

III.

1.   i)   c

ii)   d

iii)   b

iv)   Above the main altar, a stained-glass window shows Christ and His apostles
partaking in their last supper together before His crucifixion and
triumphant resurrection from the dead.

v)   d

vi)   A 1942 letter from Mr. Irving Grey, alumnus of the orphanage, states that,
many of the children "made good" in life, one of the boys becoming the
rector of a church in North Carolina. "For this," continues the letter, "many
of us are mighty thankful."

2. Christian Character Traits:

a. selflessness
b. devotion
c. dedication
d. Christian love
e. protection of the helpless
f. thankfulness
g. industriousness
h. usefulness
i. helpfulness
j. guarding the reputation of others

LESSON 7

III.

1. i) c

   ii) d

   iii) *Senate* and *Justice*, symbolizing our legislative and judicial system of government and showing forth from whence our power is derived.

   iv) c, f

   v) c

   vi) b

   vii) b, e, f

   viii) The Word of God. Composed by Thomas Jefferson, it begins with an acknowledgment that man's freedom and equality was bestowed upon him by Almighty God.

   ix) We hold these truths to be self-evident, that all men are created equal, that they are endowed by their Creator with certain unalienable rights, that among these are life, liberty and the pursuit of happiness. . .appealing to the Supreme Judge of the world,. . .declare, That these United Colonies are, and of right ought to be, free and independent states. . .And for the support of this Declaration, with a firm reliance on the protection of Divine Providence, we mutually pledge to each other our lives, our fortunes and our sacred honor.

   x) c

xi) d

xii) All legislative powers herein granted shall be vested in a Congress of the United States, which shall consist of a Senate and House of Representatives.

xiii) The ratification of the conventions of nine states shall be sufficient for the establishment of this Constitution between the States so ratifying the same.

xiv) Done in Convention by the unanimous consent of the States present the seventeenth day of September in the year of our Lord [Jesus Christ] one thousand seven hundred and eighty-seven, and of the independence of the United States of America the twelfth. In witness whereof we have hereunto subscribed our names.

GEORGE WASHINGTON

xv) c

xvi) b, d

xvii) c, e

2. *Christian Character Traits:*

a. Extolling Almighty God
b. Dependence upon God
c. Acknowledging God's Sovereignty
d. Recognizing the impartiality of God
e. Constitution signed "in the year of our Lord [Jesus Christ]"

f. God, the giver of life
g. God, the giver of liberty
h. God, the giver of happiness
i. The Divinity of God
j. The Justice of God

LESSON 8

III.

1. i) b

   ii) c

   iii) The function of Memorial Stamps is to honour great people of caliber; worthwhile achievements; anniversaries, expositions and historical events of great significance.

iv)   c, e, g, h

v)   c

vi)   The Apollo 8 mission which first put men into orbit around the moon. Colonel Frank Borman, Captain James Lovell and Major William Anders were the astronauts on this lunar expedition. For the first time in history, the Word of God was relayed back to planet earth from the moon.

vii)   d

viii)   b

ix)   c

x)   c

xi)   b

xii)   d

xiii)   b

xiv)   a

xv)   c

2.   *Christian Character Traits:*

a.   godliness (Scripture read from the moon)
b.   hospitality (*Dove of Peace* weathervane)
c.   perseverance (Gutenberg Bible printing)
d.   praise to Almighty God
e.   diligence (Gutenberg Bible printing)
f.   extolling God's Sovereignty
g.   celebration of Christ's birth
h.   acknowledging God
i.   Trust in God
j.   extolling the power of prayer (George Washington praying in Valley Forge)

LESSON 9

III.

1. i)   b

   ii) c

   iii) d

   iv) The purpose and function of the Organization of American States is the establishment and maintenance of a forum for the peaceful cohabitation of nations in the western hemisphere.

   v)   c

   vi) Daniel's identity as Old Testament prophet of God who predicted the four great world Empires and the seven years' Great Tribulation.

   vii) d

   viii) Isabella holds a pomegranite in her hands, from which a dove, symbol of the Holy Spirit, takes flight.

   ix) This is the Statue of Queen Isabella of Spain and the Americas who sent Christopher Columbus to discover the New World. Donated by Spain to the Organization of American States. April 14, 1966. Day of the Americas.

   x)   d

2. *Christian Character Traits:*

    a.   acknowledgment of sin (Daniel the prophet)
    b.   confession of sin (Daniel the prophet)
    c.   repentance for sins (Daniel the prophet)
    d.   humility (Daniel the prophet)
    e.   extolling God's righteousness (Daniel the prophet)
    f.   self-sacrifice (Isabel of Spain)
    g.   dedication (Daniel the prophet)
    h.   reliance upon the Holy Spirit's guidance (Isabel of Spain)
    i.   perseverance (Christopher Columbus)
    j.   courage (Christopher Columbus)

LESSON 10

III.

1.   i)   d

      ii)   On *The Fourth Day*, God created the vault of the sky and He made the sun, and the moon, and the stars to shed their light upon the earth.

      iii)   On *The Fifth Day*, God created the fish of the sea, the birds of the air and the beasts of the dry land.

      iv)   On *The Sixth Day*, God created mcn.

      v)   On *The Seventh Day*, God rested.

      vi)   In the beginning, God created the heavens and the earth.

      vii)   a) *The First Day*, the Spirit of God brooded over the waters.
             b) *The Second Day*, God separated the light from the dark.
             c) *The Third Day*, God created the earth.
             d) *The Fourth Day*, God created the vault of the sky, and He made the sun and the moon and the stars to shed their light on the earth.
             e) *The Fifth Day*, God created the fish of the sea, the birds of the air and the beasts of the dry land.
             f) *The Sixth Day*, God created men.
             g) *The Seventh Day*, God rested.

      viii)   Nothing was more characteristic of President John F. Kennedy than his support of the arts in America. . .He believed that through its artists, its poets, musicians, painters, dramatists, a society expressed its highest values.

      ix)   The Eisenhower Theater, with approximately 1,100 seats; the Opera House, with a capacity for 2,200 persons, the Concert Hall, accommodating 2,700 people and the Terrace Theater, seating 500 theatergoers.

      x)   c

      xi)   d

      xii)   b, e

      xiii)   b, d

xiv)   Sing for joy to God our strength
        Shout joyfully to the God of Jacob
        Raise a song, strike the timbrel
        The sweet sounding lyre with the harp
        Blow the trumpet at the new moon
        At the full moon on our feast-day
        For it is a statute for Israel
        An ordinance for the God of Jacob

xv)   Praise Him with the sound of trumpet
        Praise Him with the psaltery and harp
        Praise Him with timbrel and dance
        Praise Him with stringed instruments and organs
        Praise Him upon the loud cymbals
        Praise Him upon the high sounding cymbals

   2.   *Christian Character Traits:*

   a.   diligence   f.   truth
   b.   perseverence   g.   godliness
   c.   excellence   h.   honor of God
   d.   steadfastness   i.   praise of God
   e.   industriousness   j.   glory to God

LESSON ONE
TEACHERS' GUIDE

5 CLASS SESSIONS
Union Station and The Christopher Columbus
Memorial Fountain

What you will need:

1. Text: Lesson 1 - The Christian Heritage of our Nation History Curriculum
    - Landmarks.
2. Illustrations (attached).
3. "The Christian Heritage of our Nation" - *Ten National Landmarks #1 video.*
4. A VCR player.
5. Thumb tacks or scotch tape.

I. Opening Activities:

Affix the following enlarged illustrations to the walls of your classroom:
(Permission is granted per teacher of *The Christian Heritage of Our Nation History
Curriculum* course of study, to enlarge the attached illustrations for display upon the
walls of a classroom.)

a) *Union Station and the Christopher Columbus Memorial Fountain.*
b) *The Christopher Columbus Memorial Fountain and Statue.* (In front of Union
    Station, Washington, D.C.)
c) Front facade of Union Station - *Thou hast put all Things under his Feet.*
    (Psalm 8:6b)
d) Front facade of Union Station - *The Truth shall Make you Free.* (John
    8:32b)
e) Front facade of Union Station - *The Desert shall Rejoice and Blossom as the
    Rose.* (Isaiah 35:1b)

Write upon a chalk board Christopher Columbus' theme Scripture verse in his
Book of Prophecies - "to bring the Gospel to Unknown Coastlands" (Isaiah 66:19)

The above illustrations are to be displayed prior to your students' arrival.
Attention should be focused upon the Christian themes inherent in the architecture
and sculpture of this major national landmark memorializing Columbus' famous voyage
and discovery of America. Allow your students the liberty to ascertain what these
visual reenactments of America's history and heritage depict.

II. Textual Reenactment: (30 minutes allotted)

Select passages from the text on the original writings of Christopher Columbus, reenacting these events through his own words. The aim of this lesson is to portray the discoverer of America in his true light, leading your students to come to their own conclusion regarding the authentic Christian identity of Christopher Columbus; that is, to prove for themselves that Christopher Columbus' life was governed by Scripture and prayer.

III. Visual Reenactment: *(15 minutes allotted)*

a) Alert your students to the fact they will now be seeing the visual reenactment of the Christian themes in the architecture and sculpture of this major national landmark, together with the narrated text, affirming Christopher Columbus' identity as the discoverer of America.

b) Play, at the first Class Session, "The Christian Heritage of our Nation" - *Ten National Landmarks #1 video.* (First Landmark)

IV. Forum Discussion, Questions, Clarifications and Answers: *(15 minutes allotted)*

a) Allow your students free rein in discussing their prior concepts, ideas and views on Christopher Columbus, Discoverer of America, from current textbooks, articles and television productions; comparing them to the above Lesson One Plan (I). Select Passages from the original writings of Christopher Columbus, together with the visual reenactments of the Christian themes depicted in the architecture and sculpture of this foremost national landmark.

b) Answer all questions pertaining to the above lesson clearly, concisely and accurately, based upon your thorough study, knowledge and understanding of Christopher Columbus' true Christian identity and commitment to Jesus Christ and His Great Commission, from the original texts provided.

c) Assign Lesson 1 Text, together with PUPILS' GUIDES (attached) to your students for critical analysis and reflective study. These should be completed and returned prior to Lesson 2.

d) Before closing the lesson, ask your students to reflect upon the question: "From the original historical writings of Columbus presented, and the visual reenactments of the Christian themes depicted in the architecture and sculpture of this foremost national landmark, was his first allegiance to God, or to gold?"

LESSON TWO

TEACHERS' GUIDE

5 CLASS SESSIONS
The U.S. Capitol - Legislative
Branch of our Government

What you will need:

1. Text: Lesson 2 - The Christian Heritage of our Nation History Curriculum - Landmarks.
2. Illustrations (attached).
3. "The Christian Heritage of our Nation" - *Ten National Landmarks #1 video.*
4. A VCR player.
5. Thumb tacks or scotch tape.

I. *Opening activities:*

Affix the following illustrations to the walls of your classroom:

a) East Steps - U.S. Capitol.
b) *The Genius of America* sculpture.
c) *The Christopher Columbus Bronze Doorway* sculpture.
d) *Christopher Columbus leaving the Convent of La Rabida* sculpture.
e) *Landing of Columbus, 1492* frieze.
f) *The Signing of the Declaration of Independence* painting.
g) *Surrender of Lord Cornwallis at Yorktown, Virginia, October 19th, 1781* painting.
h) *Scene at the Signing of the Constitution of the United States* painting.
i) *Moses* bas-relief sculpture, U.S. House of Representatives.
j) *George Washington kneeling in Prayer at Valley Forge* stained-glass window.

Write out upon a chalk board Psalm 16:1:

Preserve me O God, for in thee do I put my trust.

The above illustrations are to be displayed prior to your students' arrival. Attention should be focused upon the Christian meaning and significance of these major landmarks of America's history, prominently displayed in the art, sculpture and architecture of our U.S. Capitol.

Allow your students the liberty to ascertain what these visual reenactments of our nation's history and heritage depict.

II. Textual Reenactment: *(30 minutes allotted)*

Select passages from the text on the original meanings of these visual master-pieces, from the artists' and sculptors' own interpretations. The aim of this lesson is to portray the historical events depicted in each work of art, in their true light, leading your students to come to their own conclusion regarding the authentic Christian identity woven into the warp and woof of the U.S. Capitol, Legislative Branch of our government.

III. Visual Reenactment: *(15 minutes allotted)*

a)   Alert your students to the fact they will now be seeing the visual reenactments of a number of these Christian events, together with the narrated text, memorialized for all Americans at a national historic site of foremost significance.

b)   Play, at the first Class Session, "The Christian Heritage of our Nation" - *Ten National Landmarks #1 video*. (Second Landmark).

IV. Forum Discussion, Questions, Clarifications and Answers: *(15 minutes allotted)*

a)   Allow your students free rein in discussing their prior concepts, ideas and views on the history and heritage of America, from current textbooks, articles and television productions, comparing them to the above Lesson Two Plan (II). Select passages from the text on the *Presidential Inaugural Scriptures* and on the original meanings of these visual masterpieces, from the great master artists' and sculptors' own interpretations, in this national historic landmark.

b)   Answer all questions pertaining to the above lesson clearly, concisely and accurately, based upon your thorough study, knowledge and understanding of the text provided.

c)   Assign Lesson 2 Text, together with PUPILS' GUIDES (attached), to your students for critical analysis and reflective study. These should be completed and returned prior to Lesson 3.

d)   Before closing the lesson, ask your students to reflect upon the question: "From the original texts presented, and the visual reenactments of the authentic history and heritage inherent in the art, sculpture and architecture of the U.S. Capitol, is America's first allegiance to God, or to politics?"

LESSON THREE
TEACHERS' GUIDE

3 CLASS SESSIONS
The U.S. Supreme Court -
Judicial Branch of our Government

What you will need:

1.　Text:　Lesson 3 - The Christian Heritage of our Nation History Curriculum
- Landmarks.
2.　Illustrations (attached).
3.　"The Christian Heritage of our Nation" - *Ten National Landmarks #1 video.*
4.　A VCR player.
5.　Thumb tacks or scotch tape.

I.　*Opening activities:*

Affix the following illustrations to the walls of your classroom:

a)　The Supreme Court of the United States.
b)　*The Contemplation of Justice* sculpture.
c)　*The Ten Commandments* on main doorway to Inner Courtroom.
d)　*The Ten Commandments* bas-relief sculpture above the Bench.
e)　*Good - The Struggle between Good and Evil with Good Prevailing* sculpture.
f)　*Evil - The Struggle between Good and Evil with Good Prevailing* sculpture.
g)　*Evil - Lies and Deceit* sculpture.
h)　*Good Prevailing - The Triumph of Justice* central panel sculpture.
i)　*Justice the Guardian of Liberty* sculpture.

Write upon a chalk board Galatians 5:22-23, reflecting *Good*; from Adolph Weinman's masterpiece sculpture: *The Struggle between Good and Evil with Good Prevailing.*

The above illustrations are to be displayed prior to your students' arrival. Attention should be focused upon the Christian meaning and significance of these predominant sculptural masterpieces within and without the U.S. Supreme Court. Allow your students the liberty to ascertain what these visual reenactments of America's history and heritage depict.

II. Textual Reenactment: (30 minutes allotted)

Select passages from the text on the original meanings of these visual masterpieces, from the artists' and sculptors' own interpretations.

The aim of this lesson is to portray the historical events depicted in each work of art in their true light, leading your students to come to their own conclusions regarding the authentic Christian identity woven into the warp and woof of the U.S. Supreme Court.

III. Visual Reenactment: (15 minutes allotted)

a) Alert your students to the fact they will now be seeing the visual reenactments of a number of these Christian events, together with the narrated text, memorialized for all Americans at a national historic site of foremost significance.

b) Play, at the first Class Session "The Christian Heritage of our Nation" - *Ten National Landmarks #1 video*. (Third Landmark)

IV. Forum Discussion, Questions, Clarifications and Answers: (15 minutes allotted)

a) Allow your students free rein in discussing their prior concepts, ideas and views on the history and heritage of America, from current textbooks, articles and television productions; comparing them to the above Lesson Three Plan (III). Select passages from the text, and on the original meanings of these visual masterpieces, from the artists' and sculptors' own interpretations, in this national historic landmark.

b) Answer all questions pertaining to the above lesson clearly, concisely and accurately, based upon your thorough study, knowledge and understanding of the text provided.

c) Assign Lesson 3 Text, together with PUPILS' GUIDES (attached), to your students for critical analysis and reflective study. These should be completed and returned prior to Lesson 4.

d) Before closing the lesson, ask your students to reflect upon the question: "From the original texts presented and the visual reenactments of the authentic history and heritage inherent in the art, sculpture and architecture of the U.S. Supreme Court; is America's first allegiance to God, or to the rulings and decisions of modern-day secular lawmakers?"

LESSON FOUR

TEACHERS' GUIDE

3 CLASS SESSIONS
The Library of Congress
Largest Repository of Americanism

What you will need:

1. Text: Lesson 4 - The Christian Heritage of our Nation History Curriculum - Landmarks.
2. Illustrations (attached).
3. "The Christian Heritage of our Nation" - *Ten National Landmarks #1 video.*
4. A VCR player.
5. Thumb tacks or scotch tape.

I. *Opening activities:*

Affix the following illustrations to the walls of your classroom:

a) The Library of Congress Thomas Jefferson Building.
b) *The Torch of Learning* atop the Library of Congress dome.
c) Sculptured face of *Benjamin Franklin*, above Library of Congress Main West Entranceway.
d) Main Vestibule - Library of Congress Thomas Jefferson Building.
e) *Nature is the Art of God* - Library of Congress Main Vestibule.
f) *There is but One Temple in the Universe and that is the Body of Man*, Library of Congress Main Vestibule.
g) *How Charming is Divine Philosophy* - Library of Congress Main Vestibule.
h) The Gutenberg Bible - 1455 A.D.
i) The Giant Bible of Mainz - 1453 A.D.
j) The Main Reading Room - Library of Congress.
k) *Religion* - Library of Congress Main Reading Room.
l) *Moses and The Ten Commandments* - Library of Congress Main Reading Room.
m) *Paul, Apostle to the Gentiles* - Library of Congress Main Reading Room.
n) *Science* - Library of Congress Main Reading Room.
o) *Judea - Religion*, Library of Congress Main Reading Room.

Write out upon a chalk board Micah 6:8 and Psalm 19:1 (Scripture verses depicting *Religion* and *Science*, inscribed upon the inner walls, Library of Congress Main Reading Room).

The above illustrations are to be displayed prior to your students' arrival. Attention should be focused upon the Christian meaning and significance of these major landmarks of America's history, prominently displayed in the art, sculpture and architecture of the Library of Congress 1897 Thomas Jefferson building. Allow your students the liberty to ascertain what these visual reenactments of our nation's history and heritage depict.

II. Textual Reenactment: *(30 minutes allotted)*

Select passages from the text on the original meanings of these visual master-pieces, from the artists' and sculptors' own interpretations. The aim of this lesson is to portray the historical events depicted in each work of art, in their true light, leading your students to come to their own conclusion regarding the authentic Christian identity woven into the warp and woof of the Library of Congress 1897 Thomas Jefferson building.

III. Visual Reenactment: *(15 minutes allotted)*

a) Alert your students to the fact they will now be seeing the visual reenactments of a number of these Christian events, together with the narrated text, memorialized for all Americans at a national historic site of foremost significance.

b) Play, at the first Class Session "The Christian Heritage of our Nation" - *Ten National Landmarks #1 video*. (Fourth Landmark)

IV. Forum Discussion, Questions, Clarifications and Answers: *(15 minutes allotted)*

a) Allow your students free rein in discussing their prior concepts, ideas and views on the history and heritage of America, from current textbooks, articles and television productions, comparing them to the above Lesson Four Plan (IV). Select passages from the text, and on the original meanings of these visual masterpieces, from the great master artists' and sculptors' own interpreta-tions, in this national historic landmark.

b) Answer all questions pertaining to the above lesson clearly, concisely and accurately, based upon your thorough study, knowledge and understanding of the text provided.

c) Assign Lesson 4 Text, together with PUPILS' GUIDES (attached), to your students for critical analysis and reflective study. These should be completed and returned prior to Lesson 5.

d)   Before closing the lesson, ask your students to reflect upon the question: "From the original texts presented and the visual reenactments of the authentic heritage and history inherent in the art, sculpture and architecture of the Library of Congress 1897 Thomas Jefferson building, does America's national library glorify God, Christ and the Bible; or computer discs and print-outs?"

LESSON FIVE
TEACHERS' GUIDE

5 CLASS SESSIONS
The White House - Executive Branch of our Government

What you will need:

1. Text: Lesson 5 - The Christian Heritage of our Nation History Curriculum - Landmarks.
2. Illustrations (attached).
3. "The Christian Heritage of our Nation" - *Ten National Landmarks #1 video.*
4. A VCR player.
5. Thumb tacks or scotch tape.

I. Opening activities:

Affix the following illustrations to the walls of your classroom:

a) The White House, North facade.
b) The White House, South facade.
c) Gilbert Stuart's famed 1796 painting of George Washington.
d) Gilbert Stuart's portrait from Christ Church's 1920 handbook.
e) John Adams' Prayer inscribed on the State Dining Room mantel.
f) George Washington's Sunday Morning and Evening, hand-written Prayers.

Write out upon a chalk board, Genesis 49:22-25c.

> Joseph is a fruitful bough, even a fruitful bough by a well; whose branches run over a wall: The archers have sorely grieved him and shot at him, and hated him: But his bow abode in strength, and the arms of his hands were made strong by the hands of the mighty God of Jacob; (from thence is the Shepherd, the Stone of Israel;) Even by the God of thy father, who shall help thee; and by the Almighty, who shall bless thee with blessings of heaven above. . .(Excerpted from George Washington's presidential inaugural Scripture).

The above illustrations and writings are to be displayed prior to your students' arrival. Attention should be focused upon the Christian meaning and significance of these major landmarks of America's history, prominently portrayed in the art, architecture and writings pertaining to the White House, Executive Branch of our government.

Allow your students the liberty to ascertain what these visual reenactments of our nation's history and heritage depict.

II. Textual Reenactment: (30 minutes allotted)

Select passages from the text on our first and second presidents' prayers, together with the original meanings inherent in the art, inscriptions and architecture of the White House, Executive Branch of our government. The aim of this lesson is to portray the historical events reflected in the founding fathers' writings, and in the artists' own interpretations, leading your students to come to their own conclusions regarding the authentic Christian identity of our first two presidents - woven into the history and heritage of the White House.

III. Visual Reenactment: (15 minutes allotted)

a) Alert your students to the fact they will now be seeing the visual reenactments of a number of these Christian events, together with the narrated text, memorialized for all Americans at a national historic site of foremost significance.

b) Play, at the first Class Session, "The Christian Heritage of our Nation" - *Ten National Landmarks #1 video*. (Sixth Landmark)

IV. Forum Discussion, Questions, Clarifications and Answers: (15 minutes allotted)

a) Allow your students free rein in discussing their prior concepts, ideas and views on the history and heritage of America, from current textbooks, articles and television productions; comparing them to the above Lesson Five Plan (V). Select passages from the text on the original writings of our founding fathers, and from the great master artists' own interpretations, in this national historic landmark.

b) Answer all questions pertaining to the above lesson clearly, concisely and accurately, based upon your thorough study, knowledge and understanding of the text provided.

c) Assign Lesson 5 Text, together with PUPILS' GUIDES (attached), to your students for critical analysis and reflective study. These should be completed and returned prior to Lesson 6.

d) Before closing the lesson, ask your students to reflect upon the question: "From the original texts presented and the visual reenactments of the authentic heritage and history inherent in the art, inscriptions and architecture of the White House, is America's first allegiance to God, Christ and the Bible, or to politics?"

LESSON SIX
TEACHERS' GUIDE

I CLASS SESSION
"The Church of the Presidents"

What you will need:

1. Text: Lesson 6 - The Christian Heritage of our Nation History Curriculum - Landmarks.
2. Illustrations (attached).
3. "The Christian Heritage of our Nation" - *Ten National Landmarks #1 video*.
4. A VCR player.
5. Thumb tacks or scotch tape.

I. Opening activities:

Affix the following illustrations to the walls of your classroom:

a) *The Church of the Presidents* on Lafayette Square.
b) *The Resurrection Window* in the *Church of the Presidents*.

Write out upon a chalk board:

"One hour every day shall be devoted to the Lord - a ruling of the guild of St. John's Orphanage, *The Church of the Presidents*."

The above illustrations are to be displayed prior to your students' arrival. Attention should be focused upon the Christian meaning and significance of these major landmarks of America's history. Allow your students the liberty to ascertain what these memorials of our nation's history and heritage depict.

II. Textual Reenactment: (30 minutes allotted)

Select passages from the text on the original meanings of these memorials, from the history of *The Church of the Presidents* and President Chester Arthur's gift to the church. The aim of this lesson is to portray the historical significance of *The Church of the Presidents* in its true light, leading your students to come to their own conclusion regarding the authentic Christian identity woven into the warp and woof of *The Church of the Presidents*.

III. Visual Reenactment : *(15 minutes allotted)*

a)   Alert your students to the fact they will now be seeing the visual reenactments of this national historic site of foremost significance.

b)   Play "The Christian Heritage of our Nation" - *Ten National Landmarks #1 video.* (Seventh Landmark)

IV. Forum Discussion, Questions, Clarifications and Answers: *(15 minutes allotted)*

a)   Allow your students free rein in discussing their prior concepts, ideas and views on the history and heritage of America, from current textbooks, articles and television productions; comparing them to the above Lesson Six Plan (VI) text on the original history of *The Church of the Presidents* recorded for posterity.

b)   Answer all questions pertaining to the above lesson clearly, concisely and accurately, based upon your thorough study, knowledge and understanding of the text provided.

c)   Assign Lesson 6 Text, together with PUPILS' GUIDES (attached), to your students for critical analysis and reflective study. These should be completed and returned prior to Lesson 7.

d)   Before closing the lesson, ask your students to reflect upon the question: "From the original texts presented, and the visual reenactments of the authentic history and heritage inherent in the art and annals of *The Church of the Presidents*, is America's first allegiance to God, or to the modern-day secular humanists' *view* of God?"

LESSON SEVEN
TEACHERS' GUIDE

5 CLASS SESSIONS
The National Archives

What you will need:

1. Text: Lesson 7 - The Christian Heritage of our Nation History Curriculum - Landmarks.
2. Illustrations (attached).
3. "The Christian Heritage of our Nation" - *Ten National Landmarks #1 video.*
4. A VCR player.
5. Thumb tacks or scotch tape.

I. *Opening activities:*

Affix the following illustrations to the walls of your classroom:

a) The National Archives building.
b) The Statue *Heritage.*
c) Seal of the National Archives - *The Ten Commandments* (Exodus 20).
d) Seal of the National Archives - *Jus* (Justice).

Write out upon a chalk board:

> "The Heritage of the Past is the Seed that brings forth the Harvest of the Future." (Inscription upon the base of the statue *Heritage*, in front of The National Archives).

The above illustrations and writings are to be displayed prior to your students' arrival. Attention should be focused upon the Christian meaning and significance of these major landmarks and symbols of America's history, prominently portrayed in the sculpture, art and architecture of our National Archives.

Allow your students the liberty to ascertain what these visual reenactments of our nation's history and heritage depict.

II. *Textual Reenactment: (30 minutes allotted)*

Select passages from the enclosed text on the original meanings of these historic documents and visual masterpieces, from the authors,' artists' and sculptors' own interpretations. The aim of this lesson is to portray the historical events depicted in each famous document; and the symbolism in each work of art, in their true light, leading your students to come to their own conclusions regarding the authentic Christian identity of America.

III. Visual Reenactment: (15 minutes allotted)

a) Alert your students to the fact they will now be seeing a visual reenactment of the architecture and sculpture of this national landmark, together with the narrated text, memorialized for all Americans at a national historic site of foremost significance.

b) Play, at the first Class Session, The Christian Heritage of our Nation - *Ten National Landmarks #1 video.* (Eighth Landmark)

IV. Forum Discussion, Questions, Clarifications and Answers: (15 minutes allotted)

a) Allow your students free rein in discussing their prior concepts, ideas and views on the history and heritage of America, from current textbooks, articles and television productions; comparing them to the above Lesson Seven Plan (VII). Select passages from the text on the original *Declaration of Independence*, *U.S. Constitution* and *U.S. Bill of Rights*, and from the great master artists' and sculptors' own interpretations, in this national historic landmark.

b) Answer all questions pertaining to the above lesson clearly, concisely and accurately, based upon your thorough study, knowledge and understanding of the text provided.

c) Assign Lesson 7 Text, together with PUPILS' GUIDES (attached) to your students for critical analysis and reflective study. These should be completed and returned prior to Lesson 8.

d) Before closing the lesson, ask your students to reflect upon the question: "From the original texts presented and the visual reenactments of the authentic heritage and history inherent in the documents, sculpture, inscriptions and architecture pertaining to our National Archives, (largest repository of White House documents), is America's first allegiance to God, or to the fluctuating whims and fancies of current occupants of the Executive Branch of our government?"

LESSON EIGHT

TEACHERS' GUIDE

2 CLASS SESSIONS
Bureau of Engraving and Printing

What you will need:

1. Text: Lesson 8 - The Christian Heritage of our Nation History Curriculum - Landmarks.
2. Illustrations (attached).
3. Tracing paper - 10 sheets per student.
4. Thumb tacks or scotch tape.

I. *Opening activities:*

Affix the following illustrations to the walls of your classroom:

a) Bureau of Engraving and Printing.
b) *Earthrise* NASA photograph, 1969 Commemorative Postage Stamp.
c) *The Gutenberg Bible,* 500th Anniversary 1952 Commemorative Stamp.
d) *The Nativity Scene* by John Singleton Copley, 1976 Christmas Stamp.
e) The Washington side of the one dollar note; the reverse sides on the two, and five dollar notes - *The Signing of the Declaration of Independence* and *The White House.*
f) *The Dove of Peace* Christmas Stamp.

Write upon a chalk board Genesis 1:1 (Scripture read back from the moon to the earth by the Apollo 8 lunar expedition): "In the Beginning God created the heavens and the earth. . ."

The above illustrations are to be displayed prior to your students' arrival. Attention should be focused upon the Christian meaning and significance of these historic events and landmarks, commemorated in the engravings, prints, portraits and art reproduced at our national Bureau of Engraving and Printing.

Allow your students the liberty to ascertain what these visual reenactments of our nation's history and heritage depict.

II. *Textual Reenactment: (30 minutes allotted)*

Select passages from the text on these items memorializing and commemorating historic events of foremost significance to our nation. The aim of this lesson is to study the historical events, portraits of the founding fathers and major landmarks of America's history, in their true light, leading your students to come to their own conclusion regarding the authentic Christian emphasis and identity woven into the warp and woof of our national Bureau of Engraving and Printing.

III. *Visual Reenactment:* *(15 minutes allotted)*

a) Alert your students to the fact they will now be tracing the following illustrations: b); c); d); e) and f), for their better understanding and grasp of these historical events.

b) At the first Class Session distribute tracing paper (10 sheets per student). Allow your students to creatively reproduce these great landmarks of Christian heritage and history for themselves.

IV. *Forum Discussion, Questions, Clarifications and Answers:* *(15 minutes allotted)*

a) Allow your students free rein in discussing their prior concepts, ideas and views on the history and heritage of America, from current textbooks, articles and television productions, comparing them to the above Lesson Eight Plan (VIII). Select passages from the text, depicting the Great Master artists' own interpretations of famous landmarks of Christian history.

b) Answer all questions pertaining to the above lesson clearly, concisely and accurately, based upon your thorough study, knowledge and understanding of the text provided.

c) Assign Lesson 8 Text, together with PUPILS' GUIDES (attached) to your students for critical analysis and reflective study. These should be completed and returned prior to Lesson 9.

d) Before closing the lesson, ask your students to reflect upon the question: "From the original texts presented and the visual reenactments of the authentic heritage and history inherent in the predominant commemorative engraving, printing and artistic reproductions of the Bureau of Engraving and Printing; is America's *first* allegiance to God, Christ and the Bible, or to monetary exchange?"

LESSON NINE

TEACHERS' GUIDE

I CLASS SESSION
The Organization of American States

What you will need:

1. Text: Lesson 9 - The Christian Heritage of our Nation History Curriculum - Landmarks.
2. Illustrations (attached).
3. "The Christian Heritage of our Nation" - *Ten National Landmarks #1 video*
4. A VCR player.
5. Thumb tacks or scotch tape.

I. Opening Activities:

Affix the following illustrations to the walls of your classroom:

a) The Organization of American States.
b) The Statue of Queen Isabel of Spain.
c) The Statue of Daniel the Prophet.

Write out upon a chalk board Daniel's prayer for his people:

> Alas, O Lord, the great and awesome God, who keeps His covenant and lovingkindness for those who love Him and keep His commandments, we have sinned, committed iniquity, acted wickedly, and rebelled, even turning aside from Thy commandments and ordinances. Moreover, we have not listened to Thy servants the prophets, who spoke in Thy name to our kings, our princes, our fathers, and all the people of the land. Righteousness belongs to Thee, O Lord, but to us, open shame. . .
>
> Daniel 9:4b-7a

The above illustrations are to be displayed prior to your students' arrival. Attention should be focused upon the Christian meaning and significance of these major landmarks of America's history, prominently portrayed in the sculpture and architecture of the Organization of American States.

Allow your students the liberty to ascertain what these visual reenactments of our nation's history and heritage depict.

II. Textual Reenactment: *(30 minutes allotted)*

Select passages from the text on the original meanings of these historic events and visual masterpieces, from the sculptors' own interpretations. The aim of this lesson is to portray the historical events depicted in each famous work of art in their true light, leading your students to come to their own conclusions regarding the authentic Christian identity of America.

III. Visual Reenactment: *(15 minutes allotted)*

a) Alert your students to the fact they will now be seeing a visual reenactment of the architecture and sculpture of this national landmark, together with the narrated text, memorialized for all Americans at a national historic site of foremost significance.

b) Play "The Christian Heritage of our Nation" - *Ten National Landmarks #1 video*. (Ninth Landmark)

IV. Forum Discussion, Questions, Clarifications and Answers: *(15 minutes allotted)*

a) Allow your students free rein in discussing their prior concepts, ideas and views on the history and heritage of America, from current textbooks, articles and television productions, comparing them to the above Lesson Nine Plan (IX). Select passages from the text on the original meanings of these masterpieces in architecture and sculpture, from the great master artists' own interpretations depicted at this national historic landmark.

b) Answer all questions pertaining to the above lesson clearly, concisely and accurately, based upon your thorough study, knowledge and understanding of the text provided.

c) Assign Lesson 9 Text, together with PUPILS' GUIDES (attached) to your students for critical analysis and reflective study. These should be completed and returned prior to Lesson 10.

d) Before closing the lesson, ask your students to reflect upon the question: "From the original texts presented and the visual reenactments of the authentic heritage and history inherent in the symbolism, architecture and sculpture of the Organization of American States, is America's first allegiance to God, or to politics?

LESSON TEN

TEACHERS' GUIDE

2 CLASS SESSIONS
The John F. Kennedy Center
for the Performing Arts

What you will need:

1. The Holy Bible (King James Version).
2. Text: Lesson 10 - The Christian Heritage of our Nation History Curriculum - Landmarks.
3. Illustrations (attached).
4. "The Christian Heritage of our Nation" - *Ten National Landmarks #1 video.*
5. A VCR player.
6. Thumb tacks or scotch tape.

I. *Opening Activities:*

Affix the following enlarged illustrations to the walls of your classroom:

a) The John F. Kennedy Center for the Performing Arts.
b) *The First Day of Creation* tapestry.
c) *The Second Day of Creation* tapestry.
d) *The Third Day of Creation* tapestry.
e) *The Fourth Day of Creation* tapestry.
f) *The Fifth Day of Creation* tapestry.
g) *The Sixth Day of Creation* tapestry.
h) *The Seventh Day of Creation* tapestry.
i) *Psalm 150* sculpture.
j) *The Israelites play Musical Instruments to the glory of God* painting.
k) *King David playing the Harp* painting.
l) *Miriam dancing and playing the Tambourines* painting.
m) *The Israelites praising God* painting.
n) *Joshua and his Followers Blowing Rams' Horns* painting.

Write upon a chalk board Genesis 1:1-3; 26-27:

> In the beginning God created the heavens and the earth. And the earth was formless and void, and darkness was over the surface of the deep and the Spirit of God was moving over the surface of the waters. Then God said, "Let there be light"; and there was light. . .Then God said, "Let Us make man in Our image, according to Our likeness; and let them rule over the fish of the sea and over the birds of the sky and over the cattle and over all the earth, and over every creeping thing that creeps on the earth."

And God created man in his own image, in the image of God he created him; male and female He created them.

II. Textual Reenactment: (30 minutes allotted)

Read Genesis, Chapter 1, slowly and meaningfully from the King James Version of the Holy Bible. Then read the following captions written by John Coburn for each of the seven *Creation* tapestries in the John F. Kennedy Center for the Performing Arts, pointing to each Day's tapestry as you read it:

a) *On the First Day*, the Spirit of God brooded over the waters.
b) *On the Second Day*, God separated the light from the dark.
c) *On the Third Day*, God created the earth.
d) *On the Fourth Day*, God created the vault of the sky and He made the sun and the moon and the stars to shed their light on the earth.
e) *On the Fifth Day*, God created the fish of the sea, the birds of the air and the beasts of the dry land.
f) *On the Sixth Day*, God created men.
g) *On the Seventh Day*, God rested.

III. Visual Reenactment: (15 minutes allotted)

Alert your students to the fact they will now be seeing the visual reenactments of a number of these artistic and sculptural masterpieces, together with the narrated text in a national historic landmark of foremost significance.

Play, at the first Class Session, "The Christian Heritage of our Nation" *Ten National Landmarks #1 video.* (10th Landmark)

IV. Forum Discussion, Questions, Clarifications and Answers: (15 minutes allotted)

a) Allow your students free rein in discussing their prior concepts, ideas and views on The Creation of the world from public, and non-public school text-books, articles and television productions, comparing them to the true Genesis Creation of the universe by Almighty God, found in the Holy Bible and depicted in *The Creation* tapestries, in America's National Performing Arts Center. Select passages from Lesson 10 Plan (X) text on The Christian Heritage of our Nation History Curriculum - Landmarks.

b) Answer all questions pertaining to the above lesson clearly, concisely and accurately, based upon your thorough study, knowledge and understanding of the Genesis account of Creation, and the correct, biblical sequence of God's Creation of His universe found in the texts provided. Assign Lesson 10 text, together with PUPILS' GUIDES (attached), to your students for critical analysis and reflective study. These should be completed and returned prior to the end of this course of study.

c) Before closing the lesson, ask your students to reflect upon the question: "From the Holy Bible's text and the visual reenactments of *The Creation* aubusson tapestries, in The John F. Kennedy Center for the Performing Arts, what is the original true sequence of events in God's *Seven Days of Creation* of His universe?"

ADDENDUM

GOODNESS

Do not look for wrong and evil, —
You will find them if you do;
As you measure for your neighbor,
He will measure back to you.

Look for goodness, look for gladness,
You will meet them all the while;
If you bring a smiling visage
To the glass, you meet a smile.
                    - Alice Carey

TRUTH

Truth is a gem so bright
That naught with it can vie.
That which but looks like truth
Is but a vile, dull lie.

GOOD ADVICE

Whatever you are, be brave;
The liar's a coward and slave,
Though clever at ruses
And sharp at excuses,
He's a sneaking and pitiful knave.

Whatever you are, be frank, —
'Tis better than money and rank;
Still cleave to the right,
Be lovers of light,
Be open, above board, and frank.

Whatever you are, be kind;
Be gentle in manners and mind;
The man gentle in mien,
Words and temper, I ween,
Is the gentleman truly refined.

Easy and pleasant 'tis to quote
The brave, bold words another wrote;
But he who rank and file would lead,
Should prove his courage by his deed.

TIME

Time is the sand of life;
And when we waste a grain
And wish to get it back, —
We can but wish in vain.

LIFE

Life is no dream or thing of naught.
But know you this, that life is thought,
And to live is not life, if naught is
wrought.

THE STARS AND STRIPES

I would cut a piece from an evening sky,
Where the stars were shining through,
And use it just as it was on high,
For my stars and field of blue.

Then I'd take a part of a fleecy cloud,
And some red from rainbow bright,
And put them together side by side,
For my stripes of red and white.

We shall always love the "Stars and
Stripes,"
And we mean to be ever true
To this land of ours and the dear old
flag,
"The Red, the White, and the Blue."

Then hurrah for the flag! Our country's
flag,
Its stripes and white stars, too;
There's not a flag in other lands
Like our own "Red, White, and Blue."

THE PIN AND THE NEEDLE

A pin and a needle were neighbors in a workbasket. Both being idle, they began to quarrel, as idle people are very likely to do. "I should like to know," said the pin, "what you are good for, and how you expect to get through the world without a head." "What is the use of your head," replied the needle sharply, "if you have no eye?" "What is the use of your eye, if there is always something in it?" asked the needle. "Yes, but you will not live long, for you have always a stitch in your side." "You are a poor, crooked thing!" cried the needle. "And you are so proud that you can't bend without breaking," answered the pin. "I will pull your head off, if you insult me again," said the needle. "I will pull your eye out, if you touch me," snarled the pin. "Remember, your life hangs by a single thread."

While they were quarreling thus, a little girl came into the room. She began sewing something hard, but soon broke the needle at the eye, and threw it under the grate. Then the girl picked up the pin. It was so crooked that it bent almost double when she tried to use it. So she threw the pin into the ashes with the needle.

"Well, here we are," said the needle. "We have nothing to quarrel about now," said the pin. "It seems that misfortune has brought us to our senses." "It is a pity that we had not come to them sooner," said the needle. "We are much like many men who quarrel about their blessings till they lose them."

(In your own words, tell the meaning of: "A stitch in your side;" "so proud that you can't bend without breaking;" "your life hangs by a single thread.")[64]

About The Author

Dr. CATHERINE MILLARD is the founder and president of Christian Heritage Tours, Inc. and Christian Heritage Ministries. She has spent fourteen years as a scholar at the Library of Congress, researching the authentic Christian history and heritage of the United States. In 1995, she was elected to "Who's Who among students in American Universities and Colleges" for outstanding academic achievement in the realm of Christian education. Dr. Millard is also the recipient of the 1990 George Washington Honor Medal and the 1992 Faith and Freedom Religious Heritage of America Award, for significant contributions in affirming and strengthening the biblical principles in American life.

She is the author of books on America's original history, to include *The Rewriting of America's History*, *A Children's Companion Guide to America's History* and *Great American Statesmen and Heroes;* as well as six video documentaries on the subject. Dr. Millard has lectured and taught the original Christian heritage and history of America extensively in colleges, universities and schools throughout the nation.

Catherine Millard is also available to provide teaching seminars, lectures and multimedia presentations to your school or organization, on the subject of America's Christian heritage and history. You may contact her through the following address:

Christian Heritage Ministries
6597 Forest Dew Court
Springfield, Virginia 22152
or call (703) 455-0333

FOR ADDITIONAL COPIES OF
THE CHRISTIAN HERITAGE OF OUR NATION HISTORY CURRICULUM - LANDMARKS
call or write Christian Heritage Ministries or go to your local Christian bookstore.
(703) 455-0333